Stories &
OLD BIRM.

This collection of stories ...ippets of
Old Birmingham is taken from a comprehensive
volume compiled by
Robert K Dent published in 1880.
The volume is entitled
"Old and New Birmingham:
A History of the Town and its People".

Edited by

Dawn G Robinson-Walsh

AURORA
PUBLISHING

ISBN: 1 85926 036 0

Published by: Aurora Publishing.
Distributed by: Aurora Enterprises Ltd,
                 Unit 9C,
                 Bradley Fold Trading Estate,
                 Radcliffe Moor Road,
                 Bradley Fold,
                 BOLTON   BL2 6RT
                 Tel: 0204 370753/2
                 Fax: 0204 370751

Edited by: Dawn G Robinson-Walsh.
                 from: "Old and New Birmingham
                 -History of the Town and its
                 People." *by Robert K. Dent, 1880.*

Printed and bound by:
                 Manchester Free Press,
                 Unit E3,
                 Longford Trading Estate,
                 Thomas Street,
                 Stretford,
                 Manchester M32 0JT.

Front cover illustration:
                 The Town Hall, Birmingham.

*Dedicated to my family, and friends made at
Lordswood Girls' School, 1970-1977.
Thanks to Sharon Shipperbottom for help with
typing and editorial work.*

OLD BIRMINGHAM

This collection of stories and snippets of old Birmingham is taken from a comprehensive volume compiled by Robert K Dent published in 1880. The volume is entitled "Old and New Birmingham: A History of the Town and its People", and contains nearly two hundred illustrations from the most authentic sources. Unfortunately, this excellent book, perhaps too detailed for many tastes, is not widely available and not a little expensive.

In this collection of selected and edited tales, I hope that we have chosen the most interesting aspects of life in old Brummagem, and have included the stories of some of Birmingham's famous sons, such as William Hutton, Matthew Boulton, and Joseph Priestley. The book also includes some detail on the rise of the institutions of Birmingham: the schools, the gaol, the asylum and perhaps more pleasantly, the parks. There are also occasional moments of drama: Birmingham's infamous rioting, a notorious murder, and events of a more literary and cultural nature.

Despite being a Brummie born and bred, having spent eighteen or so years of my life in Winson Green, my birthplace, there were a number of facets to Birmingham's history of which I was unaware - for example, that Winson Green was not so very long ago called Birmingham Heath. Hopefully, the narrative and pictures will act as an informative and entertaining collection of Birmingham miscellany for the inhabitants of this great city.

Dawn G Robinson-Walsh.
1994.

CONTENTS

NOSTALGIC
POSTCARD BOOKS

Other books in the

Stories & Tales

series...

Stories and Tales of
Old Manchester

Selected and Edited by
CLIFF HAYES

Stories and Tales of
Old Merseyside

Selected and Edited by
CLIFF HAYES

Stories and Tales of
Old Lancashire

Selected and Edited by
CLIFF HAYES

STORIES & TALES OF
OLD YORKSHIRE

Originally edited by William Smith in 1883

Selected & Edited by Dawn Robinson-Walsh

ILLUS:- THE EAST PROSPECT OF BIRMINGHAM ABOUT 1730.

1

ORIGINS OF THE CITY

Birmingham is a city which has grown of centuries, but its early history as a once insignificant Warwickshire town is little known. By its industry, and the ingenuity of its inhabitants, Birmingham developed to become famous throughout the world as home to the arts, the birthplace of many useful inventions and as a centre of intellectual and political liberty.

At the beginning of the 16th Century, Birmingham was described by Leland as a little village of one street. It has since developed into a great metropolis, but no thanks to pompous ceremony, royal visits, decrees, edicts and the like. Industrial progress has been its making. The Domesday Book tells us: "Richard holds of William four hides (a hide was about 50 acres) in Bermingham. The arable employs six ploughs; one is in the demesne. There are five villeins and four bordons, with two ploughs. Wood half a mile long and four furlongs broad. It was and is worth 20s".

THE NAME OF BIRMINGHAM

The development of the name Birmingham is a bone of contention. Apparently, there are at least 140 different ways of spelling the word. William Hutton, misled by the common corruption of the name into Brommigeham or Brummagem, believed the original to have been Bromwych (Brom from broom, the shrub, for which the soil is very favourable, and Wych, a dwelling). Once prosperous, its lord might assume its name, reside in it and the particle ham (Bromwych's ham) would follow.

However, from the Domesday Book, the name is Bermingeham or Bermingham. The word Birmingham is thought to be Saxon. The final syllable, ham, means a

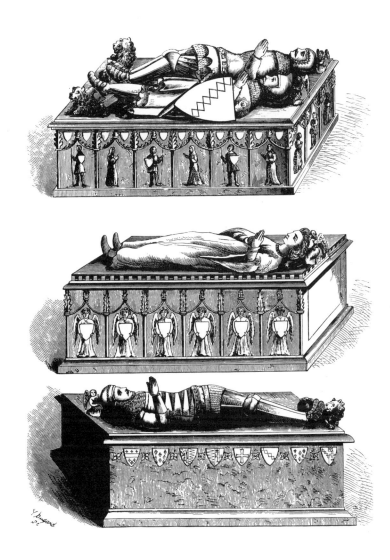

ILLUS:- MONUMENTS OF THE BERMINGHAM
FAMILY.

home or residence and Bermingham would be a family name meaning the Berms (from Berm) and ing or inng, the young offspring, race or tribe. Brummagem probably arose from the old local pronunciation of the soft g as in "singe".

Some historians have tried to link the place with the Roman station, Bremenium, as an important hardware station, but this is more fancy than fact. The Romans did pass near to the place–see the name of Icknield Street and some traces of the road remained in Icknield Port Road and Sutton Park.

FIRST IMPRESSIONS OF BIRMINGHAM, AROUND 1837, BY A TRAVELLER FROM KENT/SURREY

"The coachman points out, amid a gloomy cloud in front of us, the dim outline of the steeples and factory chimneys of Birmingham. On down the wide open roadway of Deritend, past the many–gabled "Old Crown House", through the only really picturesque street in Birmingham, Digbeth, up the Bull Ring, round the corner into New Street, where we pull up at "The Swan".

Bull Street was then the principal street in Birmingham for retail business and it contained some very excellent shops. Carrs Lane had a very narrow opening, and the Corn Exchange was not built. Most of the courts and passages in High Street were filled with small dwelling houses, and the workshops of working bookbinders. The narrow footpaths and contracted roadway were inconvenient.

New Street was not much more lively than Newhall Street. The Grammar School and the Theatre were unaltered between the 1830s and 1870s, externally, "The Hen and Chickens" remained the same and the Town Hall was not finished.

On New Street was the office of the "Birmingham Journal" which originally started as a Tory paper by a few "old fogies". "The Times" had, early in 1825, in a leader, held up to well-deserved ridicule some action on the part of the Birmingham Tory Party. At a meeting, a well-fed, prosperous-looking, fox-hunting iron merchant from Great Charles Street, rose and moved that "The Times" had disgraced itself and insulted Birmingham and that it was the duty of every Birmingham man to stop its circulation in the town. A copy of the paper was ceremoniously burned to ashes. It was there and then decided to start a local Tory newspaper.

The Town Hall had been opened for three years, but was incomplete. Nearly opposite was a wretched architectural failure "The School of Medicine". Bennetts Hill was considered THE street of the town, architecturally. In St Philip's Churchyard, there was a low fence and pleasant avenues of trees on the sides next to Colmore Row and Temple Row. The bells would chime out every three hours and it was a quiet walking place for evening.

The Workhouse stood about half way down Lichfield Street. It was a quaint pile of building, probably about 150 years old. There was a large quadrangle, low two-storey buildings and a high brick wall next to the street.

There was little of note until Aston Park in the Aston Road. The park was then entire and completely enclosed by a high wall, similar in character to the portion in the Witton Road. The Hall was occupied by the second James Watt, son of the great engineer. The village of Aston was as country-like as if located twenty miles from a large town. Perry Barr was a terra incognita to most Birmingham people. Erdington, then universally called "Yarnton" was little known and Sutton Coldfield was a far-off pleasant spot for picnics-but, to the bulk of Birmingham people, as much unknown as if it had been in the New Forest.

Broad Street was skirted on both sides by private houses, each with its garden in front. Rice Harris lived in the house which is now the centre of the Children's Hospital and the big, ugly "cones" of his glass factory at the back belched forth continuous clouds of black smoke. Beyond the Five Ways, there were no street lamps. The Hagley Road had a few houses dotted here and there. All along the straightened part of it there was, on the left, a wide open ditch, filled generally with dirty water. The "Plough and Harrow" was an old-fashioned roadside public house. Calthorpe Street was pretty well filled with buildings. St George's Church was about half built. Frederick Street and George Street (for they were not roads then) were being gradually filled up but the greater proportion of Edgbaston was agricultural land.

The south side of Ladywood Lane was pretty well built upon, owing to its being the nearest land to the centre of the town not burdened with town rating. Further to the east was Icknield Street, near the canal bridge, which at that time was an iron one, narrow and very dangerous.

Soho Park from Hockley Bridge for about a mile on the road to West Bromwich was entirely blocked in. The factory built by Boulton and Watt had an original engine put up by James Watt. From Hockley Bridge to the corner of Livery Street, many of the houses had a pretty bit of garden in front and were mostly inhabited by jewellers. The whole area of the Great Western Railway was then covered with buildings, and small streets ran through to Snow Hill.

There were only around ten churches in Birmingham. St Geoerge's Church looked clean and new. In May, 1933, Birmingham was visited by a very severe epidemic of influenza, and few households escaped.

Horses were also attacked by it, and the proprietor of "The Hen and Chickens" lost by death sixteen horses in one day.

By 1837, Birmingham had grown from a large and populous but ugly town, to as handsome as any town in England. In almost the centre of the country, it was a great centre commercially, artistically, politically, and intellectually. It became a vast metropolis with an energetic and far-seeing Municipal Council. Its merchants were known and honoured throughout the world. Its manufactured products were necessities to nearly every member of the human race-it became the second city of the Empire".

RAIL TRAVEL TO BIRMINGHAM IN THE 1830s

Railway travelling then was in a very primitive condition. Except at the termini, there were no platforms. Passengers had to clamber from the level of the rails by means of iron steps, to their seats. The roof of each of the coaches was surrounded by an iron fence or parapet, to prevent luggage from slipping off. First class carriages were built upon the model of the inside of old stage coaches. They were so low that even a short man could not stand upright. The seats were divided by arms, and the floor was covered afresh for each journey with clean straw. The second-class coaches were simply execrable, with the sides utterly unprotected from the weather. When the weather was wet, or it was snowing, it was truly horrible, and according to the testimony of medical men, was the primary cause of many deaths.

A PUBLIC HANGING

This is an account of the first and only public execution within the boundaries of the town. A watchman pacing Snow Hill during the night of July 18th, 1806, questioned a suspicious character who shot him by pistol and mortally wounded him. A man called Philip Matsell was accused of the crime, arrested and found guilty. He was condemned to be hanged at the spot where the deed was committed.

On August 22nd, a strange and grim sight was witnessed in the busy streets of Birmingham, such as had never been seen in the town before. A gibbet was erected near the bottom of Snow Hill, at the junction with Great Charles Street, with a scaffold. Large crowds of the idle, dissolute and curious turned out to see the sight. A crowd met the coach containing the criminal at Camp Hill and greeted Matsell with shouts and hisses.

He was brought out in the middle of the crowd, pinioned by the executioner with cords, in sight of everyone, placed in an open cart covered with black, and with his coffin before him, the hangman on one side and a clergyman on the other, the procession passed through Deritend to Snow Hill.

There was a dense crowd of nearly 50,000 people–some jeering and cursing and some sobbing and hysterical; the only calm person was said to be the condemned. He spurned all spiritual consolation and practical assistance, and leaped in the air with a "here goes", as he was suspended on a gibbet 20ft high.

RIOTS IN THE CITY

After the passing of the Reform Bill in 1832, there was a political lull in England for a few years. The middle classes, being satisfied with the success they had achieved for themselves, did not trouble themselves very much for the extension of the franchise to the working classes. So long as trade remained, and wages were easily earned, the masses remained quiet, but the disastrous panics of 1837 altered the state of affairs: trade was depressed, bad harvests and the Corn Laws meant dear bread, wages fell, work became scarce and manufacturing in many places entirely closed.

Naturally enough, the working men attributed their sufferings to their want of direct political influence and clamoured for the franchise, spurred on by the demagogue, Feargus O'Connor.

In 1838, half a dozen MPs united with a like-size group of working men to compose "The People's Charter", with six main demands for the working classes: universal suffrage, vote by ballot, equal electoral districts, annual Parliaments, abolition of the property qualification for MPs, and payment of Members.

In Birmingham, meetings were held every Monday evening at Holloway Head, then an open space. On 13th August, 1838, there was a huge demonstration of (reputedly) 100,000 people. A petition in favour of the charter received nearly 95,000 signatures. Torchlight meetings were held almost nightly throughout the country and Government prohibited them.

Birmingham remained quiet until early April, 1839. On 13th May, a number of delegates called themselves the "National Convention" and assembled in Birmingham. Their object was to frighten Parliament into submission to their demands. They recommended a run for gold upon the savings banks, abstinence from excisable articles and universal cessation from work.

It was rumoured that a general rising in the Black Country had been arranged for a certain day with hundreds of pikes already forged, plus formidable weapons which consisted of four spikes of pointed iron, about 4 inches long, from a common centre, with one spike uppermost however thrown. People were afraid to venture out after nightfall.

On Friday, 29th June, the Mayor, William Scholefield, met the mob and tried to induce them to disperse, promising the use of the Town Hall once a week if they would refrain from meeting in the streets. The mob marched noisily through New Street, Colmore Row, Bull Street, High Street and the Bull Ring.

The following Thursday, the group met again in great force at the Bull Ring with flags, banners and insignia. Without notice, a large body of London police, having arrived by train, came out of Moor Street and rushed at the mob. A terrible fight commenced. The police fought their way to the standard bearers and demolished the flags. In a short time, the Bull Ring was nearly cleared. The people rallied, with improvised weapons and returned to the attack. The police were outnumbered, surrounded and rendered powerless. Some were stoned, others knocked down and badly kicked, some beaten badly about the head and some stabbed.

A magistrate arrived, the Riot Act was read, and the military occupied the Bull Ring. Seven police had to be taken to hospital; one was stabbed in the abdomen, another in the groin. About one dozen rioters were arrested and found to be armed with deadly weapons and had large stones in their pockets. The mob grew and headed off to Holloway Head, where they pulled down twenty yards of the railing of St Thomas's Church, arming themselves with iron bars. They proceeded to "The Golden Lion" in Aston Street and disappeared.

On Monday, 15th June, the Bull Ring filled after the petition asking that the Charter become law was rejected and some of the leaders were committed for trial. The crowd became so dense that the shops were closed in case windows may be accidentally broken. At 8 o'clock, an organised gang of hundreds in number, armed with bludgeons, iron bars and other weapons, marched up Digbeth. They turned down Moor St and attacked every window of the Public Office. On the way to the Bull Ring, they fell upon a respectable solicitor named Bond, who happened to be passing and left him for almost dead. Iron bars were use as battering-rams against shop doors. Messrs. Bourne's shop, at the corner of Moor Street, was the first to give way and was looted. Iron railings were pulled down at St Martin's and bars of iron surrounding Nelson's monument.

Leggatt's upholstery, in the Bull Ring, was broken and set on fire. By 9 o'clock, many shops were on fire. There was also a blazing pile in the street. Shops were freely entered and robbed. Women and children ran away laden with costly goods of all kinds, as the men urged each other on.

At 10 o'clock, a troop of Dragoons came from the High Street, with swords drawn and at full gallop. They had been ordered to strike with the flats only, but after stones were thrown at them, some rioters got some nasty cuts. One hundred police joined in.

Many arrests were made and the prison in Moor Street was soon filled. Barriers, guarded by soldiers, were placed at the entrances to all streets leading up to the centre of town. 2,000 special constables were called into active service.

The next morning, the shops in all the principal streets were closed. From Moor Street to about 100 yards beyond New Street, there was scarcely a whole pane of glass left. Most doors and shutters were in splinters. Some buildings were still smoking and steaming. The west side of the Bull Ring from "The Spread Eagle" to New Street was in a similar condition but there had been no fires.

The day after the riots, a letter bearing the previous day's London postmark arrived at Messrs. Bourne:

"The people shall rise like lions and shall not lie down till they eat the prey, and drink the blood of the slain under JESUS CHRIST,
Taking vengeance upon all who disobey
THE GOSPEL".

It is therefore assumed that the riots were planned from outside and premeditated. What happened to the rioters?

Three men, Howell, Roberts and Jones, and a boy named Aston were found guilty of arson and condemned to death. The jury recommended them to mercy but the judge did not support this. The Town Council petitioned for remission, and the inhabitants of the area sent a separate petition-the first signatures being of Messrs. Bourne. They were ultimately transported for life. Many others were released and about a dozen were sentenced to various terms of imprisonment with hard labour. The cost of claims for the damage amounted to £16,283.

BULL BAITING

The following is the last reference in a local journal, Aris's Gazette, sent on October 12th, 1835. It was a letter to the editor.

Sir,

It must be gratifying to every friend of humanity, that during the last Session of Parliament, a bill, the provisions of which, if strictly enforced, will have the effect of abolishing the horrid and demoralising practice of Bull-Baiting, was introduced and received the Royal Assent. It therefore behoves the Ministers and Churchwardens of those parishes where the cruel system has been pursued, to avail themselves of the power now placed in their hands, and zealously to carry into effect the humane intentions of the framers and supporters of the bill, while every sincere friend to humanity will cheerfully lend his assistance.

As an individual deeply interested in promoting the happiness of the brute creation, I shall devote my time and labour in this good cause, and exert myself to render the bill effectual to the end designed. For want of such exertion, Bull-baiting was carried on to a horrible extent during the last wake at Brierley Hill, and thousands of people from distant parishes congregated together to enjoy this feast of blood.

Three bulls were then baited on the Saturday evening previous to the wake Sabbath, and for four successive days they were torn and lacerated for their amusement in a manner too shocking to relate. Trusting that the diabolical sport will be speedily abolished, I remain, Sir, your obliged servant.

Brierley Hill, October 3rd, 1835.

COCK-FIGHTING

The amusements of our ancestors would now be viewed with loathing and disgust at the cruelty and brutality which seems to have pervaded most popular sports. Events such as cock-fighting, bull-baiting and dog-fighting are to be found in the columns of old newspapers, as calmly reported as we now write about cricket or football.

The place most famous for these brutal pastimes was Duddeston Hall. The nature of the adverts was as follows:

June, 1746. "This is to give notice that there will be a Main of Cocks fought at Duddeston Hall, near

13

Birmingham, betwixt the Gentlemen of Warwickshire and Worcestershire, for 4 guineas a Battle, 40 guineas the Main. To weigh on Monday, 9th, June and fight the two following days."

Cock fights would often use hundreds of birds and go on for days.

Regular cock-fights were seen as entertainment-county matched against county and town against town. The higher classes attended these as enthusiastically as the poorer. They often lasted several days and excited more interest and attention than politics.

The "new pit in Smallbrook Street" became the favourite scene for these fights and it was not closed until between 1825 and 1830. On one occasion, magistrates seized a hundred or so spectators and principals, tied them together and marched them through the streets as an example. Badger-baiting and bear-baiting also survived, but in a lesser degree. These animals were kept for the purpose, and one great black bear called "Old Nell" kept by a person in Coleshill Street was celebrated on account of its great skill in defending itself.

THE NEW STREET THEATRE

In August, 1787, the New Street Theatre seems to have been the scene of something like a playhouse riot, with bottles, plates, apples and so on thrown at the actors by those in the gallery. A reward was offered by the manager for the detection and apprehension of the offenders but nothing more is known.

The "Gazette" told of several ineffectual attempts to set fire to the New Street Theatre, but at length the plot met with success and a little after 1am on Friday, August 17th, 1792, the theatre was in flames, which "issued from the front and every part of the building, and illuminated the whole town".

All attempts to save it were fruitless; in about 4 hours, there remained nothing of the principal theatre in the town except the blackened walls. The motive for this act were not known, but the Proprietors offered a reward of 200 guineas.

The poor players were great sufferers, for loss of their wardrobes. The dresses of all of them were entirely burnt, except Mr Marshall, who intrepidly entered the dressing room and rescued his clothes from the flames. Among other suffered was the famous comedian, Suett, who was a great wig collector, who lost a large black peruke with flowing curls, said to have once been the property of Charles II. The loss of this highly-prized relic was a matter of considerable grief to the actor.

THE MYSTERIOUS MURDER OF MARY ASHFORD

In May, 1817, a crime was committed within five miles of Birmingham which aroused a good deal of interest. A pretty country girl, Mary Ashford, the daughter of a gardener living at Erdington went as usual to Birmingham on market day.

On her way, she had called at the house of Mr Machell in Erdington, where a female friend, Hannah Cox, was in service. She made an appointment to call for her on her way back, to accompany her to a dance at a public house called Tyburn House.

She sold her stock in the market and went to the house of her friend's mother, to change her dress, then set out for the dance. She was dressed in a clean, neat white print dress, and attracted many rustic admirers. One was Abraham Thornton, son of a small farmer, who danced with her all evening.

Her friend, Hannah Cox, left the house a little before midnight and waited at a nearby bridge until Mary

ILLUS:- PORTRAIT OF MARY ASHFORD.

Ashford, Abraham Thornton and a young man named Benjamin Carter joined her. The two couples started to walk to Erdington but Carter returned soon afterwards to the house. This delayed Hannah who caught up with her friends a mile further on.

Shortly after, Hannah branched towards home. At about 2am a man called John Umpage who lived near to Mary Ashford's home, heard voices in the lane, a few yards from the scene of the subsequent crime. He heard them again at around 3 o'clock. There were various sightings of Mary that night. The last person to see her alive, at around 4.20am was Thomas Broadhurst. At around 4.30am, a labourer started his walk to work. He reached Erdington at about six o'clock. He passed by on the footroad leading to Penn's Lane and noticed a bonnet, a pair of shoes and a bundle in the pit.

One of the shoes was very bloody, so he called someone else to look at it. Blood was visible in various places around. He carried on to work, having alerted others to the peculiar sight. At about 7am, the body of a young woman was dragged out of the pit with a rake- it was Mary Ashford. The dress she wore was blood-stained and on each arm were marks from a man's hands. Footprints were seen, male and female, in the soft ground of the adjoining field. Large other marks were seen indicating a struggle.

Thornton was taken into custody and searched. The search resulted in an admission of criminality but not as to the murder, and he stated that the girl had consented. Thornton, however, had testified statements as to his whereabouts at various times. It seems impossible to believe that he could have been seen in various places at different times and also managed both crimes, crossed the field and reached his destination at times required.

The trial excited the ranks of people, and a number

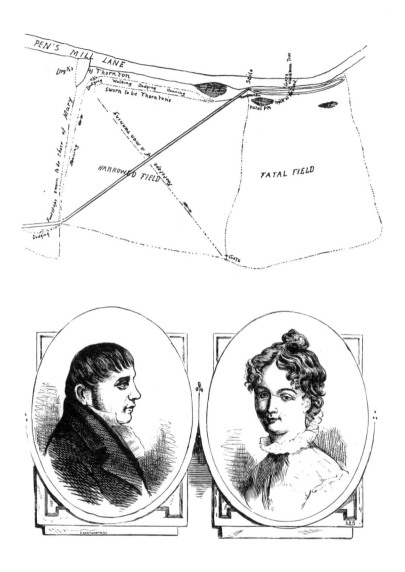

ILLUS:- PLAN OF THE SCENE OF MARY
        ASHFORDS DEATH.
        ABRAHAM THORNTON & MARY ASHFORD.

18

assembled at County Hall to hear it. The court was crowded, the jurors (mainly farmers or yeomen) were sworn in and the prisoner was charged with Mary's murder by throwing her into a pit of water. Thornton pleaded "not guilty". The jury returned a verdict of "not guilty" without retiring.

The verdict seemed most unsatisfactory to many, especially William Ashford, Mary's eldest brother. He took out a private prosecution. William was a plain, country man, about 22 years old, short, with sandy hair and blue eyes. The prisoner was asked if he was guilty. His reply was "Not Guilty, and I am ready to defend the same with my body". He produced a pair of large gauntlets, put one on his left hand in challenge and threw the other on the floor for William to take up. This was extraordinary. There had been no "wager of battel" since 1638.

Ashford was little more than a boy and much weaker physically than Thornton; it was an unfair match. The Bench were not keen on the appeal of murder, as it implied a miscarriage of justice in the trial. When the court refused to accept conclusive evidence of guilt, Ashford decided it was useless to pursue the case further and withdrew the appeal.

THE MARTYR OF DERITEND

As the 14th century drew to a close, the new doctrines of John Wycliffe began to be circulated, and Deritend and Bordesley were areas particularly keen on the new teachings and disatisfied with their parish in Aston. The great distance at which they were situated from their church often prevented the inhabitants from joining in public worship, especially in winter, when streams flooded and obstructions made the journey eventful. The people determined to build a church for themselves on their side of the River Rea.

The church was built and agreement was made that the thirteen inhabitants may appoint (at their own charge) a chaplain to administer to them. John Rogers, the first Protestant martyr during the troubled times of Queen Mary, who worked with Miles Coverdale in the translation of the Bible, received his earliest religious teaching here.

John Rogers was born in the hamlet of Deritend somewhere around the year of 1500. The honour of having given birth to the first martyr of the reign of Mary, and the editor of the first printed English Bible, was originally claimed for Birmingham by Anderson in his Annals of the English Bible.

Rogers was educated at the University of Cambridge, and was called to be a chaplain to merhants in Antwerp. Here, he met William Tyndale and Miles Coverdale, both exiled from England because of their religious convictions. The two Reformers saw in John Rogers a man of great ability who could help to translate the Bible into English. He became very knowledgeable about the gospels, and he cast off the "heavy yoke of popery, perceiving it to be impure and filthy idolatry".

He married and went to Wittenberg in Saxony, where he learned Dutch and increased his learning. After the accession of Edward VI, Bishop Ridley invited Rogers to return to England, to which he immediately responded. In 1551, he was appointed a Prebendary of St Paul's and later Dean of the College of St Paul's to the professorship of theology. On the accession of Queen Mary, he was called to preach at St Paul's Cross the first sermon after the Queen's proclaimation. He knew the danger to which his opinions exposed him under the new regime, but he proclaimed them openly and continued in the Protestant faith, exhorting people to "beware of all pestilent popery, idolatry and superstition".

For this sermon, he was immediately summoned to appear before the privy council, and he defended his conduct well, obtaining a temporary dismissal. He was recalled ten days later for the same sermon. He was then commended to remain a prisoner in his own house. After six months, he was sent, with the uncharitable help of Bonner, Bishop of London, to Newgate Prison, to be lodged among thieves and murderers. Twelve months passed during which time he was barred from all companionship, even his books, or news of his family.

He was later recalled and excommunicated. On Monday, 4th February, he prepared himself for the fire. He begged to be allowed to see his wife for a few minutes but this was cruelly refused. He was taken to Smithfield to be burned and was allowed a few words. He exhorted people "to remain in the true faith" for which he gave his life. Thus, bravely perished John Rogers, a worthy son of Birmingham.

THE OLD CROWN HOUSE

Prominent in Deritend on the Banks of the Rea was the fair "Mansion House of tymber" known as the "Old Crown House". The House (late 14th century) was built chiefly of timber and consisted of a large Central Hall, with small rooms on each side of the ground floor, and a "Great Chamber" and other rooms on the first floor.

The house has interesting associations. The "Great Chamber" became the "Gallorye Chamber". In it, according to tradition, Queen Elizabeth I passed a night. The house was positioned so as to experience and witness much of the history of the city: Prince Rupert and the gallant struggle the people made to

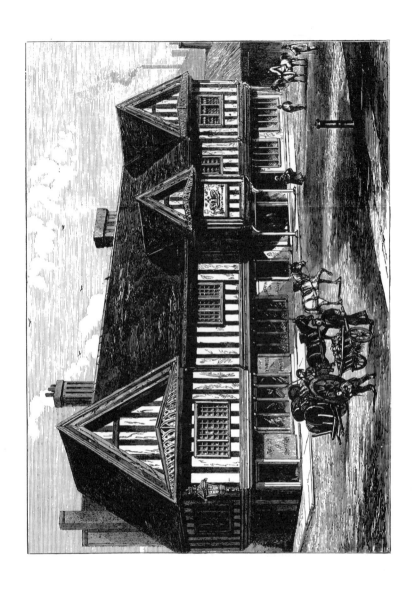

ILLUS:-"THE OLD CROWN HOUSE", DERITEND.

22

prevent his entering the town; of Shakespeare, who may have journeyed past during his early days of Warwickshire rambling; of old Leland, riding through the pretty street as he entered Birmingham. A fire blazed half a mile away from here on 14th July, 1791, when Joseph Priestley set fire to his dwelling and destroyed his invaluable philosophical library.

When Birmingham was but a village, it is easy to imagine the second William de Birmingham as he passed out to join his father in law in the rebel army of Simon de Montford.

ASTON HALL

The erection of the "noble hall" at Aston began in 1618. Sir Thomas Holte began to reside in his mansion in 1631, but it was not completely finished until 1635. The building consists of a centre and two wings, a compliment to the Queen after whom the style is called. The name of the architect is not known but it may have been one of the works of Inigo Jones.

Davidson wrote: "If the east front of Aston Hall may be designated as grand, the southern view may, with equal propriety, be termed beautiful".

The owner of Aston Hall, Thomas Holte, had a family of 15 children, the eldest of whom, Robert, died young. The second, Edward, born 1600, married one of the daughters of King James's "King of Preachers" and provoked the threat of disinheritance and was exiled from his father, until 1642, when he spent 2 nights at Aston Hall, as King Charles's army was marching from Shrewsbury to relieve Banbury Castle.

That evening was memorable in the annals of Aston Hall. The King was treated with due deference but was anxious to see if the father would treat his son with any affection. The King is believed to have said "Rejoice in thy noble mansion and thy broad domains-but remember! there is a canker at the root of all thy greatness, so long as that gallant son of thine-in so few days to shed his blood in thy royal master's cause-remains unforgiven for the magnanimous crime of having made her whom he so truly loved his wife".

Edward Holte was wounded at the Battle of Edge Hill. He recovered and remained faithful to the King but died in 1643, from a fever contracted during the defence of Oxford. In Birmingham, at the Hall, there was some alarm. The people had been cruelly treated by Prince Rupert and the Cavaliers, and seemed keen to avenge themselves. Holte had assisted the royal cause against Parliament. The Hall was armed with 40 musketeers.

On 26th December, 1,200 Parliamentary forces attacked the Hall-the number probably consisted mainly of undisciplined townsmen, with the assistance of gunners and regular soldiers. The siege continued for 3 days until the defenders surrendered, having lost 12 men and inflicting a loss of 60 on the enemy. The cannon marks are visible and the handsome staircase was damaged. The Hall was plundered, many family papers were destroyed and Sir Thomas was imprisoned and lost around £20,000.

Holte was seen as a man of obstinacy and pride, but he also showed cruel vengeance. There is a story that he once returned from hunting, and laid a bet as to the punctuality of his cook, who for once, was late. The baronet, enraged by the jeers of his companions, is said to have rushed into the kitchen and cut the cook's head in half with a cleaver. Sir Thomas escaped justice.

Sir Thomas outlived all his children, except his eldest daughter, Grace. He died at 83 and was buried in Aston Church. Perhaps Sir Thomas had some qualms of conscience about his cruelty to his son (who died in penury) and his servant, for he provided in his will for the building of an Almshouse which was to be an

ILLUS:- ASTON HALL.

asylum for the poor.

THE BATTLE OF BIRMINGHAM

A few days before the memorable Battle of Edge Hill
(23rd October), Charles I passed through Birmingham.
The day after he left the town, the inhabitants seized
his carriages containing the royal plate and other
valuables and removed them to Warwick Castle. They
also harrassed the royal party by attacking small
groups of them and sending them to prison in Coventry
–hence the proverbial expression of "sending to
Coventry". They also gave material assistance to the
Parliamentarians, supplying them with arms, such as
15,000 swords for the Earl of Essex's forces.
Early in Spring, 1643, Prince Rupert received orders
from his royal master to proceed, with a detachment of
1,200 horses and 600–700 footmen, to open a
communication between Oxford and York. The King
ordered him to march towards Lichfield and through
Bromwicham, which had a reputation for hearty, wilful,
affected disloyalty.
The inhabitants of Birmingham had already cause to
fear an attack on their towns, so decided to arm
themselves and keep two Captains for disciplining and
ordering the men. During the preparations, news came
that Prince Rupert, with around 2,000 men was
marching towards Birmingham. He reached the town at
3 o'clock on Easter Monday afternoon. The town's
entire forces amounted to only 200 men, and the Prince
did not expect resistance so a demand was made for
lodging and protection, assuring them they should
suffer no injury if they co-operated.
Soldiers and citizens joined to oppose the Prince and
discharged their shot upon him. They cursed them
calling them "develish Cavaliers and Popish Traytors"

ILLUS:- CHARLES I.

ILLUS:-GREAT STAIRCASE, SHOWING INJURIES
SUSTAINED DURING THE CANNONADING

with great commotion. They fought bravely and succeeded twice in beating off the Prince's army at the entrance to the town. Eventually, they were overpowered. The Prince, however, was still unable to enter, as the inhabitants had blocked up the deep and narrow way between Deritend and Camp Hill with carriages.

One account said the route was taken over the meadows. "The Cavaliers rode up into the Towne like many Furyes or Bedlams... they shot at every door or window where they could espy any looking out, they hacked, hewed or pistolled all they met without distinction".

Provoked by the continued resistance of the inhabitants and enraged at losing several distinguished officers, Prince Rupert gave orders to his soldiers to set fire to the town. "His wrath is said to have kindled in Bull Street". They used everything they could to kindle fire, and shot and endeavoured to kill by sword or pistol anyone that appeared to try to preserve their goods. Eighty seven houses were destroyed, plus stables and outbuildings leaving 300-400 people homeless.

Not content with setting fire to the town, they also pillaged and plundered. A local miser, Thomas Peake, was robbed of nearly £1,500 alone. They spent their last night of occupation of the town in rioting, drunkenness and debauchery.

Royalists saw the massacre as "Prince Rupert's Burning Love to England, discovered in Birmingham's Flames". The Parliamentarians saw "the town of Birmingham was unworthily opposed, insolently invaded, notoriously robbed and plundered, and most cruelly fired in cold blood the next day by Prince Rupert's Forces".

THE PLAGUE

From the ashes of the fires kindled by Prince Rupert in 1643, Birmingham seemed to have steadily risen into prosperity as a manufacturing community, but in 1665, when the Great Plague visited London and other places, Birmingham did not escape.

The infection is said to have been brought to the town in a box of clothes brought by a carrier, and lodged at an inn called the White Hart. Thereupon, the dreadful scourge followed. Houses were desolate, silence reigned in the streets, and on many doors appeared the fatal sign of the presence of the plague–a large red cross and the words "Lord have mercy upon this House". The number of victims was so great that the churchyard was insufficient to contain them and a large pit was dug on Ladywood Green, an acre of wasteland near St John's, which became known as the Pest Ground.

THE SCARCITY RIOTS

The distress of the country, caused partly by oppressive war taxation, and partly by the failure of the harvest and consequent scarcity and expense of wheat, drove many of the poorer classes to distraction, and their discontent found rent in numerous outbreaks against the millers and farmers, and the monied classes of the country. Such an outbreak happened in Birmingham in June, 1795, and led to serious and fatal results.

The cornmill and bakehouse of a Mr Pickard, at the bottom of Snow Hill, supplied the town with flour and bread. The great scarcity of grain had raised its price considerably. A poor woman complained to the maid servant of Mr Pickard that the loaf she purchased was less than usual. The maid servant answered that she was sorry about it, but wheat was now very dear, and should people not be content and not complain as they were better off than some countries–she understood from the papers that the scarcity was so great in France that the common people were reduced to eating grains.

It was quickly rumoured that Mr Pickard had said he would make the poor eat grains in their bread, and that he had buried a large quantity of corn under his mill. A mob, mainly of women, assembled round the mill and began to break the windows. Magistrates appeared but a group, urged on by furious women, made their way into the premises and threw stones and bricks at the magistrates. The Dragoons were sent for. They arrived, but not before the mob had broken into the counting house and destroyed many of Mr Pickard's accounting books. The Riot Act was read. The military speedily cleared the premises and kept the peace. Shortly after the troops dispersed, another attack was made. The troops within the mill came and arrested some of the leaders: the Constables ordered them to load their pieces before the protestors and told them that if the party conveying the arrested to the dungeon were attacked, they had orders to fire.

Within a hundred yards, a rescue was attempted. Soldiers were beaten, pelted and pressed on all sides. The soldiers slightly wounded some with their bayonets and fired shot over people's heads. This, instead of intimidating, increased their violence, and in self-defence and obedience, one Dragoon fired upon his assailants. A young man named Allen instantly fell dead and the ball which passed through his heart and body lodged deep in the chest of another who died later in hospital. The mob dispersed and peace was regained.

At the inquest, the verdict of justifiable homicide was reached. Similar riots started elsewhere but were stopped before they reached this fatal stage.

A RUNAWAY APPRENTICE

1741 was the year that William Hutton first visited Birmingham. He was born in Derby, on 30th September, 1723. In 1738, after enduring many hardships, he entered the service of an uncle, at Nottingham, as an apprentice to the trade of stocking weaving.

His uncle thought him idle and when he did not complete some set tasks one week, beat William with a broom made of heath with a hazel handle. This chastisement was semi-public. William's pride was hurt. A female acquaintance jeered at him about the beating which stung him to the quick, so he resolved to leave town.

He cut the following figure- "a lad of 17, not elegantly dressed, nearly 5ft high, with a brown linen bag containing bread and butter, a new Bible, one shirt, a pair of stockings, a sundial, a wig and a hat with 2 shillings in his pocket."

On his travels, his baggage was stolen. He arrived at Walsall and begged some beef-fat from a butcher to rub on his blistered feet. He was recommended to Birmingham to find work. On his way, he saw a curious sight-the female nail-makers of the Black Country.

Arriving on Handsworth Heath, he saw the great town. He was charmed by the beauty of St Philip's Church. These were his first impressions:-

"The environs of all I had seen were composed of wretched dwellings, replete with dirt and poverty; but the buildings in the exterior of Birmingham rose in a style of elegance. Thatch, so plentiful in other towns, was not to be met with in this. I was much surprised at the place, but more at the people. I had been among dreamers, but now I saw men awake; their very step along the street shewed alacrity".

ILLUS:- HUTTON'S FIRST VISIT TO BIRMINGHAM.

On trying to find employment, he was scorned as a runaway apprentice. Dejectedly, he walked towards the Bull Ring; two good samaritans bought him a pint and found him lodgings. Hutton was one of the first commentators on Birmingham. He returned home to his father but later became one of Birmingham's worthy citizens.

THE GENERAL HOSPITAL

As 1765 was ending, the first touch of winter led men to think of the poor, especially the sick. The rapid increase of the population of Birmingham and the danger attached to many of its occupations, rendered it necessary that some provision should be made to supply competent medical assistance for the poor. Some people pointed out that the workhouse had an infirmary attached for the poor and sick.

A local, eminent physician, Dr John Ash, resolved to build a hospital and subscriptions were welcomed. Donations soon swelled. Dr Ash selected land on Summer Lane. The building was estimated to cost £3,000 and was designed to accomodate one hundred patients. However, building work was delayed as funds ran low, and the wealthy inhabitants by 1767 were more interested in the profitable speculation surrounding the Birmingham Canal. Various fund-raising festivals were carried out.

The hospital was formally opened on 20th July, 1779, nearly 14 years after the first meeting. There were only 40 beds. In the first week, 10 in-patients were admitted, and staff were recruited at 4 guineas per annum, plus an additional guinea "if they behave well". A barber was also appointed to shave the patients twice a week.

THE RIOTS OF 1791

The decade which preceded the riots was one of great prosperity for the dissenters in Birmingham. In 1781, the Methodists completed the old meeting house in Cherry Street. Wesley visited the town and administered the sacrament to nearly seven hundred people in 1787.

The Baptists and Independents also extended their sphere of labour by erecting meeting houses. In 1789, the Roman Catholics found a home once more in the town from which they had been banished for a century. The Jews built a new synagogue in Severn Street, which was then pleasantly situated on the outskirts of town, with an almost uninterrupted view of Edgbaston's countryside. The Swedenborgians were the latest of the new sects to erect a place of worship in Newhall Street.

Dr Priestley became pastor in the area. He was seen as mild, persuasive, unaffected, with sermons of sound reasoning and good sense. While the dissenting sects were progressing, not a single new place of worship was erected in connection with the established church. This rapid growth of dissent became alarming, seen as dangerous to the welfare of the State. Dr Priestley was by no means silent on local issues nor repeal of the Corporation and Tests Acts.

Dr Priestley was seen as a major cause of the riots, firstly by sympathising with the advocates of the Revolution in France (1789). He was identified with a meeting on 14th July, 1791, at the Hotel in Temple Row, to celebrate the anniversary of the destruction of the Bastille. Most of the masses were opposed to the French Revolution.

14th July arrived and fears of a disturbance were rife. The meeting was to be postponed but the proprietor of down to dinner at 3 o'clock to toast liberty.

Their opponents, the anti-Jacobins, were holding a meeting at an inn near to the hotel. They kept up a cry of "Church and King forever". Hutton says the "rabble... would have sold their King for a jug of ale, and demolished the Church for a bottle of gin". A spy had entered the hotel and brought word that the dissenters had "cut off the King's head and set it on the table".

The mob hissed and hustled the gentlemen as they left the meeting but re-assembled at 8 o'clock and attacked the hotel, possibly in an attempt to find Dr Priestley. They then proceeded to the New Meeting House which was smashed and burned, leaving four blackened outside walls. A second party of rioters attacked the Old Meeting house which they razed to the ground. They did their utmost not to damage surrounding houses except for those of dissenters.

Another party went to attack the Swedenborgian church but their Minister told them they were loyal to the throne and government and scattered money among the throng. No damage was done.

The mob attacked the house of Priestley by breaking down doors and windows and throwing out furniture. They tore and burned the books and manuscripts in the doctor's library. His valuable library was scattered so "the high roads for a full half a mile were strewed with books".

The shrubs and trees in the garden were all trampled down or torn up. The crowd broke into the doctor's laboratory and destroyed everything before setting it on fire. One man was killed by the felling of a cornice pole. This brought the action to a close with most of the rioters sleeping or in a state of helpless intoxication in the fields around the house. The mob had found the cellar where they drank all they could drink and were up to their ankles in what they couldn't drink.

The next day, as they recovered, different parties of rioters returned into town. Business was totally suspended and all shops were closed, while on every door almost was chalked "Church and King" to provide immunity from injury. The doors of the Bridewell and other places of confinement were thrown open and the mob were joined by "the dangerous classes", parading the streets armed with bludgeons, shouting "Church and King".

The magistrates and other chief inhabitants beseeched the crowd to desist from violence but by now they were thirsty for plunder. At 2 o'clock, they attacked Baskerville House, the residence of J Ryland, Esq, a pleasantly situated mansion. The rioters were strengthened by reinforcements, bringing their number up to nearly a thousand. Every room was entered, and they remained drinking wine long after the building was fired, some even till the roof fell in. Seven people were burned to death in the cellar, one was buried in one of the vaults (and was unable to get out until the following Monday, where he expired outside on the grass) and many were taken to hospital for their scorches and bruises.

The magistrates swore in as many people as were willing as special constables. They were sent to Baskerville House, where a fierce struggle ensued and the rioters attacked them with bludgeons and stones, causing a retreat. A Mr Thomas Ashwin was so severely wounded that he died shortly afterwards.

Simultaneously came information that another party of rioters had attacked Bordesley Hall, so a second detachment of constables were sent who succeeded in driving out the rioters and kept the mob at bay, while family and valuables were moved. The mansion was, in a short time, entirely gutted.

On Saturday morning, having in addition destroyed William Hutton's place of business, they set off to his country residence at Bennett's Hill, Washwood Heath. Another party attacked the house of Mr George Humphreys at Sparkbrook.

The Huttons fled. They had reached Sutton Coldfield, but panic reached the town and they journeyed on to Tamworth where they spent the night. The following day they returned via Castle Bromwich.

The magistrates issued a handbill, explaining the cost of the damage to all these houses, and the probable extra taxation which would be brought to pay for it. So, the taxpayer in general would pay for the damage. This address failed to restore peace. The lovers of the King proceeded to pull down and burn the Meeting House at Kingswood and reduced it to ashes. Oddly, they do not seem to have entertained the slightest scruple about nonconformists' wine that they did about their houses.

The next place which required pulling down in the interests of Church and King was Edgbaston Hall, the residence of Dr Withering, but the place was saved by rumour of the words "light horse". The townspeople were welcoming to the military. It was a small troop, of sixty four in all, but sufficient to scare the rioters from their destruction.

On Monday morning, however, a fresh contingent of would-be rioters arrived, a large body of colliers from the Black Country, who wanted to join in the fray, but the military received reinforcements, too, so the miners withdrew. Before the day was over, something like order was restored and business was resumed, and although disturbing rumours of a fresh outbreak kept surfacing, it was evident that peace was at last fully restored.

Following the riots came the deluges of paper, recording and giving opinions on events. The trials of the rioters took place at the Warwick Assizes on August 2nd. Only 12 people were arraigned, and of these only 4 were convicted.

ILLUS:- HOUSES DESTROYED BY THE RIOTERS,
JULY, 1791.

One of the prisoners was a Joseph Careless. It was proved by two witnesses that he appeared to be the ring-leader in demolishing Baskerville House. He had been seen with an oak rail, 2 yards long, knocking down the brick-work of a bow-window, and driving away the pigs. However, his sister-in-law swore that he came not as a rioter, but to suppress the riot, and he let out two pigs from an outhouse which was soon after burnt down. This evidence, together with his good character-all the rioters seemed to have good characters-obtained for him his acquittal.

Four of the rioters were found guilty and received sentence of death: Francis Field, John Green, Bartholomew Fisher & William Hands. All the others were acquitted and even of the four, only two actually suffered the penalty of death.

The leniency of the Court towards these violent supporters of "Church and King" passed into a proverb. On one occasion, not long after the trial, a gentleman who was hunting with fox hounds, was so sure of killing the fox that he cried "Nothing but a Birmingham jury can save him!"

The claims of the sufferers were heard at the Spring Assizes in Warwick in 1792. The total bill of costs amounted to £35,095 13s 6d. Here, as at the trial of the rioters, the whole weight of authority was against the dissenters.

The amounts allowed in court totalled £26,961 2s 3d and were paid grudgingly "with as much reluctance as if the sufferers had destroyed their own property". The mere costs of the trial, borne by the dissenters, amounted to £13,000.

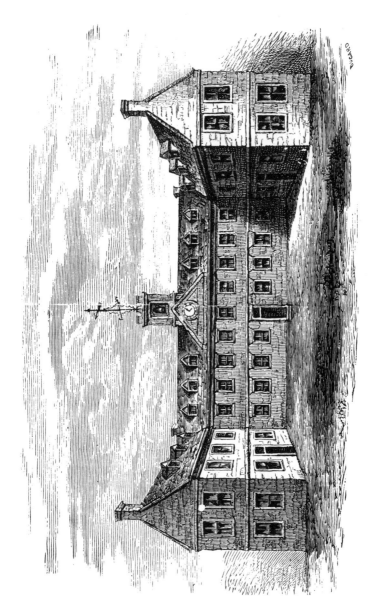

ILLUS:- THE OLD WORKHOUSE.

40

THE WORKHOUSE, THE GOAL AND THE ASYLUM

The original workhouse was an old building in Lichfield Street erected in 1733. It was a plain, substantial building, situated at the lower end of the street, built at a cost of £1,173,3s 5d.

By the mid 1800s, the old building had begun to fall into delapidated condition, and the growth of the town had rendered its site entirely unfit for such an institution. It was no longer possible to see from its windows the beautiful undulating countryside from Aston to Barr Beacon and from Erdington to Sutton Park-the view was now shut out by the wilderness of dingy brick and mortar on every side. Eventually, it was resolved that a new building should be erected on the land in the neighbourhood of the Gaol and the Lunatic Asylum. The first stone was laid on 9th September, 1850 and the building was opened on 29th March, 1852, when over 8,000 people visited it.

It was planned with some degree of care and thoughtfulness for the comfort and welfare of its inmates-all the apartments used by the aged poor were on the ground floor and every room in the building benefited from sunshine for some of the day to enhance the health and cheerfulness of the inmates. The chapel, which faced the road, was tastefully fitted and capable of accomodating 1,000 worshippers. It was built in perpendicular style and the total cost including land, furniture and building materials was £44,476.

Prior to the incorporation of the borough, all prisoners were sent to the county gaol at Warwick, and all except petty sessions cases had to be tried at the county sessions; the lock up at Moor Street was used only for the detention of prisoners awaiting the decisions of the magistrates. The entire constabulary force in the town, previous to 1838, consisted only of 19 men, to protect the lives and property of more than 150,000 inhabitants. In 1844, the Council resolved to go one step further and erect a Borough Gaol on Birmingham Heath. The Gaol was completed in 1849, the first prisoner being received on 17th October of that year.

It was built on the design of Pentonville. The building was (and still is) of brick with stone dressings, with warders' turrets on the walls, to give a castellated appearance. It was originally built to contain three hundred and thirty six cells.

On a site in the neighbourhood of the Gaol was the Borough Lunatic Asylum. The first stone was laid in September, 1847, and the building was complete by June,1850. It contained accomodation for nearly 400 inmates, and had books, newspapers and periodicals to help cure the unfortunate inmates, and also maintained well-kept grounds and gardens for the use of patients. Thus, by the mid 1800s, the welfare of most of the Borough's most unfortunate people was being taken to hand.

BRUMMAGEN GROATS

The manufacturers of Birmingham were a busy and thriving race. They boasted that their hardware was highly esteemed in London and even as far as Ireland. They had acquired a less honourable name as coiners of bad money. In allusion to their spurious groats, some Tory wit had fixed on demagogues who hypocritically affected zeal against Popery, the nickname of Birminghams.

Yet in 1685, the population was less than 4,000; Birmingham buttons were just beginning to be known; of Birmingham guns nobody had yet heard and the place did not contain a single regular shop where a Bible or almanack could be bought. On market days, a bookseller named Michael Johnson, the father of the great Samuel Johnson, came over from Lichfield and opened a stall for a few hours. This supply was long found equal to demand.

The notoriety of Birmingham in the matter of base coinage, together with the part taken by the townsmen in the civil war, caused the town to become the butt of every court wit, and her name the synonym for every species of meanness and villainy, giving birth to sayings like: "I coined heroes (by a writer) as fast as Birmingham groats".

THE LITTLE RIOT

The year 1793 was marked by a scene of disorder which caused anxiety among local inhabitants lest it should lead to a second 1791. The disturbance arose from the events of 1791 to an extent, by the refusal of certain people to pay their proportion of the levy to pay the riot bill.

The rate had been levied some time prior to the disturbance and the amount unpaid had been advanced by the local governing body on behalf of the inhabitants. On 9th September, a pressing call was made upon the ratepayers to pay in to the constables their respective amounts. One man, named Wood, of Lichfield Street, refused to pay his proportion of riot rate and it became necessary to distrain his goods for the amount. This was done on October 21st but the defaulting ratepayer resisted, threatening the lives of the officers, and soon succeeded in raising a mob which attacked the house of one of the constables, breaking windows and causing considerable damage.

By 10pm, the riot was looking so serious that one of the local magistrates, with the police and the troops of horse, found it necessary to attend to restore order. The mob, however, showed no signs of desisting. Even after the Riot Act had been read, they remained deaf to the overtures of law and order and the magistrate found it necessary to arrest the ring leaders and instruct the military to disperse the others.

Then followed a general street fight between the military and the rioters, 26 of whom were safely lodged in their Dungeon and several others were conveyed to hospital. The military kept up a presence in the streets and the night was quiet. By Tuesday, the rioters again rallied at St Philip's Churchyard. Again, the magistrates and military appeared, the Riot Act was read, and two other troops of horse arrived to rout the ratepayers.

In the afternoon, a man who had been heard to threaten, in a public house, that the prison should be pulled down that evening, was speedily lodged there himself. A mob gathered at night and attempted to force the door. The gaolers fired on them, two were severely wounded and the rest retreated. Wood, the cause of the disturbance absconded, but was arrested a few days later at Walsall. He and another rioter, Joseph Darby "the pothouse desperado who had threatened to pull down the prison" were committed to Warwick Gaol.

The second and third instalments of the riot levy appear to have been collected without serious disturbance.

COACHES AND HORSES

Although the introduction of stage coaches into England took place as early as the middle of the 17th century, they did not become popular for many years, and those who could afford to do so performed their journeys on horseback.

Coaches were seen to be a great mischief, destructive to trade and land. They were said to destroy the breed

BIRMINGHAM STAGE-COACH,

In Two *Days* and a half; begins *May* the 24th, 1731.

SET out from the *Swan-Inn* in *Birmingham*, every *Monday* at fix a Clock in the Morning, through *Warwick*, *Banbury* and *Alesbury*, to the *Red Lion Inn* in *Alderfgate ftreet*, *London*, every *Wednefday* Morning: And returns from the faid *Red Lion Inn* every *Thurfday* Morning at five a Clock the fame Way to the *Swan-Inn* in *Birmingham* every *Saturday*, at 21 Shillings each Paffenger, and 18 Shillings from *Warwick*, who has liberty to carry 14 Pounds in Weight, and all above to *pay One Penny a Pound.*
Perform d (if God permit)

By Nicholas Rothwell.

The Weekly Waggon fets out every *Tuefday* from the *Nagg's-Head* in *Birmingham*, to the Red Lion Inn aforefaid, every *Saturday*; and returns from the faid Inn every *Monday*, to the *Nagg's-Head* in *Birmingham* every *Thurfday.*

Note. By the faid Nicholas Rothwell at Warwick, all *Perfons* may be furnifhed with a *By-Coach*. *Chariot*. *Chaife*. or *Hearfe*, with a *Mourning Coach* and able *Horfes*. to any Part of *Great Britain*, at reafonable *Rates*: And alfo Saddle Horfes to be had.

ILLUS:- BIRMINGHAM EARLY COACHING BILL.

of good horses and make men careless of attending to good horsemanship. However, the stage coach became the recognised mode of travelling for over 200 years. As early as 1679, there was a Birmingham coach to London, so Birmingham people had a facility for travel which meant men could visit the metropolis and pick up new ideas.

The stage coaches were constructed principally of dull, black leather, thickly studded, with four oval windows, with heavy red wooden frames and green stuff or leather curtains. On the doors were displayed the coach's starting point and destination. The coachman would sit on a long narrow boot. Behind the coach was the immense basket attached by iron bars which seemed scarcely equal to the enormous weight with which they were often loaded.

The wheels of these old carriages were large, ill-formed and usually red, and 3 horses were usually affixed. The burden the animals dragged was unwieldy and would rock as if on heavy seas.

The slow rate at which these lumbering old coaches travelled-about 3 miles an hour-grew to be a source of disatisfaction. Improvements were made, so that by 1742, the Birmingham to London "Flying Coach" would journey from start to finish in 2½ days.

The discomfort of the jolting, rolling, lumbering coach was a drawback. The wretched condition of the roads and poor speeds afforded great opportunities for thieves. It was not an infrequent occurrence for passengers to arrive at their destination minus money and valuables, unable to pay for accomodation at an inn, or for food. Often, a traveller would make his will before embarking on a journey. Horseback was pleasanter but still left one prone to be ordered to "Stand and Deliver".

The highwaymen of the period were often romantically seen as "gentlemen". In 1750, "The Gazette" reported an incident where a Mr Henry Hunt was "stopp'd on Sutton Coldfield, in the Chester Road, by two Highwaymen, who robb'd him of his watch and his money", but on Mr Hunt asking him to give him back some silver, the Highwaymen returned him six shillings, shortly after robbed someone else to make it up and rode off!

Another highwayman stopped a coach in 1751. He behaved very civilly to passengers, told them he was a Tradesman in distress and hoped that they would contribute to his assistance. The hat was unceremoniously passed round and everyone gave something, which amounted to around £4. He was well satisfied, but returned some half pennies, saying he never took copper. He then told them there were two other collectors on the road but that he would see them out of danger, which he did.

BIRMINGHAM IN 1660

Hutton quotes an anonymous observer that "Birmingham, at the Restoration, probably consisted only of three streets". However, he believes it probably consisted of fifteen, containing about nine hundred houses. Hutton's fifteen streets comprised: Digbeth, Moat Lane (called also Court Lane), the Corn Market and Shambles, Spiceal Street (sometimes called Mercer and sometimes Spicer Street), Dudley Street, Bell Street, Philip Street, St Martin's Lane, Edgbaston Street, Lee's Lane, Park Street (from Digbeth nearly to Freeman Street), Manor Street (as far as Castle Street), Bull Street (not so high as the Minories), High Street and Deritend and Bordesley. But some of these could scarcely have been worthy of the name of streets so early as 1660.

Probably the first house the traveller reached would be

the Old Ship Inn, the traditional head-quarters of Prince Rupert in 1643 – on rising ground to the left, near to the position taken up by the townsmen in their attack on the Royalist forces, he would see the quaint half-timbered "Stratford House"; few other houses would be passed until he reached the "Old Crown". He then enters the "pretty street" called Deritend, passing St John's Chapel on the left; crosses the river Rea by the old bridge and reaches Digbeth. Deritend and Digbeth still together form the most picturesque street in the town, with many windings, and quaint old half-timbered houses.

Our traveller, proceeding up Digbeth, and after passing these picturesque old houses, would enter Cock Street, or Well Street, as the upper part of Digbeth was then called, from which he would soon reach St. Martin's church, and passing the eastern end of it, along the "Corn Cheaping" through the Shambles (which occupied the place of the present Bull Ring) and by the old Market Cross, he would reach the "High Town", the portion of High Street below the end of what was afterwards called New Street, but which was then merely the Stourbridge Road and contained few buildings except the old Free School, of timber and the Leather Hall, both of which were at the High Street end.

Beyond that point the thoroughfare was called the Beast Market and the traveller would find a few houses dotted here and there along Bull Street at the nearest end of the town, although in all probability "Bull Street" was not known by name, being perhaps merely the road out of town to Wolverhampton and Walsall, along with the armed townsmen, under Captain Greaves, were pursued by the Earl of Denbigh, in 1643. There would also be a few houses at the beginning of Dale End, the upper part of which was called "Broad Street". At the junction of these roads, which had long been called the "Welsh End", the Welsh Cross was later built, and further along the Coleshill road, at the point at which the Stafford Road branched off, was an older cross of the simplest form.

We now retrace our steps as far as the Market Cross, passing by the western end of St Martin's this time, down Mercer or Spicer Street. Turning to the right, along Edgbaston Street, our traveller would find himself on the western outskirts of the town, one of the last houses probably being St Martin's Rectory, an ancient half-timbered house, surrounded by a moat, pleasantly situated opposite the end of the road now called Dudley Street. Passing down St Martin's Lane, our traveller would, by turning to the right, down Moat or Court Lane, immediately come to the moat surrounding the ancient manorial residence of the Lords of Birmingham and this would have completed his survey of the town.

By the close of the century, Birmingham had seen considerable changes to its appearance and extent. St Martin's Church, in its ugly red brick casing would not seem to be an improvement upon the grey crumbling walls of the old church 40 years ago. There were at least seven new streets and nearly three times as many houses. There were, in the year 1700, over 15,000 inhabitants. Between High Street, New Street, Edgbaston Street and Dudley Street had grown up quite a new town, with several streets intersecting it, among them Old Meeting Street, Colmore Street and the Froggery. New Street had probably grown at least as far as Peck Lane, and Bull Street as far as the Minories. Going out in the direction of Coleshill, the houses would have extended almost to The Old Cross, while much of the ground between the part of High Street called the Beast Market and Moor Street would be filled up with dwellings.

In the town itself, there would have been fewer open spaces at the back of the houses which lined the streets, for these were now one hundred courts and alleys. But there were still green fields and pleasant gardens within easy access on every side. The upper end of Moor Street and all the land below Park Street, was yet under cultivation or used as grazing land. Behind the fringe of houses which shut in High Street from the country on the north-eastern side of the town, fields and gardens stretched out. St.Philip's Church was by then unthought of and the pleasant grassy knoll, later called Bennett's Hill, was far away from the smoke and bustle of the town and the sound of the anvil.

SAMUEL JOHNSON IN BIRMINGHAM

In the year 1733, Samuel Johnson, having found the drudgery of an ushership at Market Bosworth, too irksome to bear, accepted an invitation from his friend, Edmund Hector, a surgeon,"to pass some time" with him as his guest, at the house of Mr Warren, with whom Mr Hector lodged and boarded. Johnson had occasionally accompanied his father on his journeys to Birmingham market.

Mr Warren, Edmund Hector's landlord, was the first established bookseller in Birmingham, and finding under the rough exterior of the ex-usher such literary culture and true genius as promised to be of great use to him, became very attentive to Johnson. In his newspaper appeared the periodical essays of Samuel Johnson. Having but slender means of subsistence, and at present scarcely any settled plan of life, Johnson determined to stay in Birmingham for some considerable time. After six months with Mr Hector, he hired lodgings in another part of the town, at the house of a person named Jarvis-probably a relation of Mrs Pater, whom he afterwards married. Johnson was urged to undertake the translation and abridgment of a "Voyage to Abyssinia", written by Lobo, a Portuguese Jesuit, which Johnson mentioned as having read in the french with pleasure while at Pembroke College. The book was soon completed and published in 1735, but in those days a book bearing a provincial imprint stood only a slender chance of being favourably received. This book was published on a London imprint and was the first literary work of the author who afterwards became the chief figure in the literary history of the eighteenth century.

It was on Boswell's second visit to Birmingham when he met his future spouse, Miss Pater. She described him as "lean and lank, so that his immense structure of bones was hideously striking to the eye, and the scars of the scrofula were deeply visible. He also wore his hair, which was straight and stiff and separated behind, and he often had seemingly convulsive states and odd gesticulations, which tended to excite at once surprise and ridicule". A story told concerning his courtship which well exhibits his disregard for more sentimental dejections. The lady, it is said, refused all offers of marriage for a while, at the same time declining to give any reasons for so doing. At last, yielding to his urgent request to tell him why she had still refused, she said "an uncle of hers had been hung, and she did not wish to bring disgrace on him". "Is that all?" said Johnson "Why, though I have never had an uncle hung, I have two or three uncles who deserved it-so let's get married and say no more about that". On 9th July, 1735, the couple set out on horseback for Derby, at which place they were to be married.

ILLUS:- "BRIDEWELL"

THE OLD PRISON OF BIRMINGHAM

From the records of the old coaching days, with their pleasant associations of shady roads lined with blossoming hedgerows, of breezy commons and snug country hostelries, to the history of damp and mouldy prison-houses and their inmates is quite a contrast.

Hutton felt that the people of Birmingham had a law-abiding characteristic, due to their industry-the hand we employed in business had "less time, and less temptation, to be employed in mischief". To the absence of "idle hands" in the town may be attributed the smallness of the gaol accomodation necessary prior to 1733.

In earlier times, the lord of the manor held a tribual on his own premises, and probably a rude prison would be annexed there to, containing stocks and a whipping cross. After the fall of the Birmingham family, one of the lower rooms of the Leather Hall in New Street was used as a prison. In 1728, a private agent to the lord of the manor erased the Leather Hall and the Dungeon, erected three houses on the spot, and received their rents till 1776, when the town purchased them for £500, to open the way. Up to this time, the only entrance to New Street from the High Town had been through a narrow passage, similar to that of the entrance to Castle Street. In the days of the Leather Hall it acquired the name of the "Dungeon Entry" and this name remained for many years after the building of the houses in place of the old hall.

From 1728-1733, the town had no other place of detention for offenders, except a dry cellar, belonging to a house opposite the site of the demolished Leather Hall. On 9th September, a meeting of the inhabitants was held in the chamber over the Cross, at which it "unanimously agreed upon" that a Dungeon be forthwith erected at the Publick expense of the said

Parish, at the place commonly called Bridewell House, near Pinfold Street. This was according to Hutton, "of all bad places the worst... dark, narrow and unwholesome within, crowded with dwellings, filth and distress, with the circulation of air prevented".

This old "Bridewell" was like most of the provincial town gaols of this period. The gaol soon became too small to accomodate its numerous prisoners; in 1757, it was found necessary "to take down The Three Houses fronting Peck Lane, in order to enlarge the Prison". the building remained the only local prison until the erection of the building in Moor Street, in 1795; and was not destroyed until 1806, when the building materials were sold for £250. It has been immortalised in a little local rhyme:-

> "Spoiled the wake,
> And stole the state,
> "And took the bull to the Dungeon".

LOCAL TRADES IN THE EIGHTEENTH CENTURY

By the close of the 17th century, Birmingham was known for her works in iron, but also famous for many manufactures by which she earned the title "The Toy Shop of the world".

It is perhaps a surprise to learn the trade later centred in South Lancashire was born in Birmingham. The first thread of cotton spun by machinery was produced in the year 1700, at Sutton Coldfield, by John Wyatt, by an arrangement of rollers in a small model. The invention was put in to practical operation in Birmingham, an engine being fixed in "a large warehouse near the Well, in the Upper Priory, and turned by two asses walking round an axis". The operation never developed into a widespread success, but the fact remains that the key-stone of the great

cotton trade in England was invented in Birmingham.
John Wyatt was also the inventor of weighing machines
for carriages, carts and wagons.

The Jacobite rebellion of 1745 gave considerable
stimulus to the local trade in implements in warfare,
especially swords – During the Civil War, the
Birmingham Sword-blade manufacturer Richard Pater,
refused to supply a single weapon to The Royalists –
however, the sword-makers of the eighteenth century
willingly executed large orders for the army of "bonnie
Prince Charlie".

Occasionally, these consignments of arms for the rebels
were intercepted by the Government. In 1744, a large
chest of basket-hilted swords, sent from Birmingham
to the Belle Sauvage on Ludgate Hill, London, was
seiged and taken to the Tower; and in October of the
same year a seizure was made of two thousand
Birmingham cutlasses, which had been sent to the
Saracen's Head. No swords were ordered by the
Government, so far as it is known, until nearly the end
of the 18th century.

The gun trade was also influence by the rebellion. The
manufacture of guns was stimulated. One of the
principal fancy trades which had arisen in Birmingham
was that of manufacturing Buckles. They had been
worn as early as the 15th century, but had fallen into
disuse, and had only been revived at the period of
Revolution. They were first made at Bilston, but the
facilities for making them at Birmingham gradually
drew trade. They were generally made from a metal
called tutania, but many inferior materials were also
used pinchbeck, silverplate, and an inferior kind of
white metal called by workmen "soft tommy".

Buckles were made in various forms and sizes, from
the small buckle on the band of the hat or the knee to
the huge shoe-buckle which nearly covered the foot;
and were sold at from one shilling to five and even ten

guineas a pair. In 1790, the buckle was dethroned and the "effeminate shoe-string" took its place.

Another of the trades dependent upon fashion was that of button-making. During the early part of the 18th century the buttons worn were mainly made with the needle. During the reign of William & Mary, costumes were covered with buttons to an extravagant and ridiculous extent. Gilt buttons were an area of excellence in Birmingham manufacture.

There was a large trade growing up in the light steel toys which were then coming in to use. "Toys" has too often been a misused and misunderstood term as regards the products of Birmingham. Birmingham never, like Holland, took "pleasure in making what the children of England took pleasure in breaking". The "Toy Shop of the World" title was earned by the manufacture of jewellery- brooches, studs, bracelets, watch-chains, châtelaines, sword-hilts and other light ornaments. This was perhaps the fore-runner of the later jewellrey trade for which Birmingham became renowned.

JOHN BASKERVILLE

The history of the art of printing in Birmingham goes back to 1717. The early productions were poorly printed, with paper, ink and letter cutting being of the commonest possible quality. So long as printing was legible, beauty was not thought of. The wretchedness of the workmanship in early books and pamphlets and the desirability of producing books which were beautiful as well as useful, appears to have been impressed upon the mind of John Baskerville, a young writing-master who taught a school in the Bull Ring in 1737.

He was a native of Wolverley in Worcestershire, but

was attracted early in life to the busy and rapidly increasing town on his doorstep. He started his working life as a cutter of grave stones at his house in Moor Street.

As a teacher of writing, the beauty of his penmanship was celebrated and he possessed a taste for ornament and proportion. From stone cutting and penmanship, he turned his attention, in 1740, to japanning. In 1745, he took on a building lease, a pleasant little estate of 8 acres (on the site of Broad Street and Easy Row) and erected himself a house in the centre of it.

John Baskerville's love of letters, and his disatisfaction with the existing state of typography, led him, in 1750, to turn his attention toward the subject of producing examples of the art of printing which would bring honour to the ancient classics and on the most eminent authors. Several years were spent in experiments and upwards of six hundred pounds were sunk before he could produce a single letter to please his fastidious taste.

In 1757, he published his first work, a magnificent edition of Virgil, sold at one guinea, for which Matthew Boulton was one of the first subscribers. This was followed by the Poems of John Milton. In 1763, he issued the magnificent Cambridge Edition of the Bible, an immense folio which has been pronounced to be the finest example of typography ever produced.

These works, said Macauley, "went forth to astonish all librarians of Europe" and were highly prized for their excellence of form, elegance and sharpness of the letters, the brilliancy of the ink, and the beautiful whiteness of the paper, as compared with that of the other books of the period. Not only did he design and cast his unrivalled type, he also made his own paper, prepared his own ink, worked his own presses, and probably bound some of his own books.

He continued to produce beautiful and readable editions

of various standard works until his death, which occured on 8th January, 1775. He died childless, and the splendid printing appliances which had cost him years of labour and many thousands of pounds, failed to find a purchaser in this country and were allowed to be purchased by a literary society of Paris for £3,700, and used to print a splendid edition of the works of Voltaire.

His character and appearance are well described by Hutton - "In private life he was a humourist; idle in extreme, but his invention was of the true Birmingham model, active. He could well design, but procured others to execute. He was remarkably polite to the stranger, fond of show, a fine figure rather of the smaller size and delighted to adorn that figure with gold lace".

Baskerville's house, which became the property of Mr Ryland was partially destroyed in the Riots of 1791, but the facade of the house was still visible. When the land was laid out for wharves, in 1821, the coffin was taken up, and was found together with the contents, to be in perfect condition, and was finally re-interned in one of the catacombs under Christ Church.

PERROT'S FOLLY

In a survey of the town, carried out in 1760, it was noted that rising in the distance, beyond Easy Hill, was discernible a tall tower, built in 1758, by John Perrot. The tower was seven storeys high, and was probably originally intended as an observatory, although it was said the builder, being a keen lover of the "sport" of coursing, erected it in order to enable him, when old age prevented him from taking part in such sports, to watch others engaged in it, from the upper storeys of the tower. It has been called "Perrot's Folly" but became more generally known as "The Monument", from which name derived that of Monument Lane, later Monument Road.

WILLIAM HUTTON IN BIRMINGHAM

In February, 1750, William Hutton paid his second visit to Birmingham, this time with a view to permanent settlement in the town. Since his memorable week's journey in 1741, he had seen many changes. In 1746, his uncle had died, and the young man had turned from the stocking trade to bookbinding.

He had attempted to establish a connection as a bookseller and bookbinder at Southwell, in Nottinghamshire, which he characterised as being "as despicable as the road to it".

So, on 10th April, 1750, he returned to Birmingham, and found a half of a shop at No.6 Bull Street, for one shilling a week. It was in the same year which saw Hutton's first serious attempt as a bookseller as that in which Baskerville made his first attempt in printing.

For the first year – a year of hardship and rigid frugality he lived almost alone, without making a single acquaintance. In 1751, he found two friends in Mr Dowler, a surgeon, who lived opposite to him in Bull Street and Mr Grace, a hosier, who occupied one of the houses which blocked up the High Street end of New Street. He decided to take on the house adjoining Mr Grace's which was to let, where he pursued his business with more success.

He soon had a good trade and in addition to selling and binding books, he also commenced lending them, so may be said to have established the first circulating library in the town. He also searched for a wife, as he had been very much troubled in the management of his household affairs. One housekeeper, in his absence, sold his books for what they would bring, left the shop and got drunk with the money. Another came well recommended by a Nonconformist Minister, who assured him she would not cheat him as she feared the Lord. However, she set some dumplings to boil without water one evening and they were burned to a cinder. His sister visited him in 1751, bringing with her an intended wife for him, but the pre-arranged match fell through.

In November, 1753, he met for the first time the lady destined to become his wife, Miss Sarah Cook. In 1755 they were married in St Philip's Church. 1756 saw the birth of his daughter Catherine, who became the constant, affectionate, and solicitous companion of her father to the day of his death and remained unmarried during a life of over ninety years span.

Also in 1756, he embarked on a stationery enterprise by purchasing £200 worth of paper and hanging out a sign -"The Paper Warehouse". This department of his business he subsequently developed by manufacturing the paper himself, erecting a mill for that purpose on Handsworth Heath, but this speculation proved disastrous as he knew little of the process of paper making and had workmen who took advantage of his ignorance.

One of his mill wrights persuaded him to convert it into a corn mill, but as a miller, he was cheated on all sides. He ultimately sold the mill, and also his house, and lost in the scheme, nearly £2,000.

However, by 1763, business was again prosperous, and he began to take part in public life. He was summoned upon the Low Baliff's Jury in 1765, and in 1768 became Overseer of the Poor. In 1769, he purchased half an acre of land at Bennett's Hill, Saltley, near Washwood Heath, and built a house for himself where he resided until his death.

THE STORY OF SOHO

Matthew Boulton was a native of Birmingham born on 3rd September, 1728, who established himself on Snow Hill as a manufacturer of "toys". It has been said of him that he "would buy any man's brains", and in this lay his great secret of success. He did not expect perfection. He patiently trained people to their work and was a keen judge of character. His pleasant manners, genial temper and unflinching justice made him honoured, loved and feared, an excellent manager of a man.

In 1757, Handsworth Heath was a barren heath, occupied only by a rabbit-warren, but in that year, John Wyrley, Lord of the Manor of Handsworth, granted a lease for 99 years to Messrs. Rushton and Evans, with liberty to divert Hockley Brook and to form a pool for the requirements of a water-mill for rolling metal. In 1762, the lease was purchased by Matthew Boulton who rebuilt and enlarged the mill – however it was too small, and in 1764, the foundations were laid of the great factory which became the scene of many noble triumphs. It was completed in 1765 and consisted of four squares, with connecting ranges of workshops, capable of accomodating a thousand workmen, the cost being c.£9,000. He was joined by a Mr Fothergill and they established a design and manufacturing centre for vases, candleabra, tripods, and silver plated wares, which led to the establishment of an Assay Office in 1733.

Matthew Boulton's many projects led him to seek additional power to execute them as water power was insufficient to suit his needs, and in 1767, he erected a steam engine, on the plan of Savery. He made the acquaintance of James Watt, a mechanic in Glasgow who had perfected valuable improvements in the steam engine. Watt obtained a patent for these and came to

Soho, where Boulton's commercial sense made use of Watt's talent. Watt was a quiet, plodding Inventor, retiring in manner and nervously anxious, while Boulton was a man of the world.

Among the many manufactures to which the steam engine was found applicable was that of coining, for which purpose a mill was erected in 1778, at which, with the aid of a few boys, eight machines were worked, each capable of striking seventy to eighty-four pieces a minute. Boulton's design was to produce a coin which should be "inimitable" but his coinage was imitated by lead pennies, faced with copper. To foil this, he made his twopenny pieces exactly 2oz in weight, and eight of them measured a foot. The pennies weighed 1oz and seventeen measured two feet, and so on. Twenty tons of copper, making 716,800 pennies, were struck every week, for many months.

THE CANALS

The 1870s are memorable in the history of Birmingham as they mark the introduction of canal navigation in the locality. The inland situation of the town, and the difficulty of transporting the heavy goods manufactured here, meant that canals offered a cheaper and more expeditious mode of transit, and were suited to the requirements of the local trade.

The first English canal was undertaken by Henry I, in 1121, but for more than 500 years, no further progress was made in inland navigation until 1608, when the New River Canal was begun. The first modern canal was the Sankey Brook Canal in Lancashire, which was begun in 1755, and which proved exceedingly prosperous and useful to the district from that date. The "canal frenzy" grew with a rapidity only equalled by that of which characterised the railway projects in the nineteenth century.

Birmingham was not slow to avail herself of the new mode of transit. On 26th January, 1767, an advertisement appeared in the "Gazette", calling a meeting to take into consideration a scheme for cutting a canal through the South Staffordshire coalfield to join the Wolverhampton Canal. The meeting was held on Wednesday, January 28th, at the Swan Inn, at which a great number of local inhabitants were present. It was unanimously agreed to have the line of the proposed canal surveyed, and the celebrated engineer, Brindley, was applied to for that purpose.

By mid July, upwards of £35,000 was already subscribed towards carrying out this project and a Bill to make the canal received royal assent on 26th July. On the "agreeable news" reaching Birmingham, "the bells were set to ringing, which were continued the whole day".

The length of the canal was about twenty-two miles and the expense of making it about £70,000, divided into shares of £140 each, of which no one was allowed to purchase more than ten.

The work was hasty – the managers unable to find patience to worm around the hill at Smethwick or cut through it, wisely travelled over it, by the help of twelve locks, six to mount the summit and six to descend. The summit was said to have been 460ft above sea level, but the inconvenience of the numerous locks being a source of continued complaint, the company eventually called in the aid of Telford to remove them; hills were cut through to a perpendicular depth of more than seventy feet, and other improvements effected, so that "the aspect of this canal was not surpassed in stupendous magnificence by any similar work in the world".

The first boat-load of coals were brought to Birmingham by the canal on November 7th, 1769, the year of the Stratford Jubilee. An office for the transaction of the company's business was erected at the western end of Paradise Street (then called Paradise Row) and from the steps of which, it is said, John Wesley preached during one of his visits to the town.

THE LAMP ACT

The Lamp Act was an Act for repairing, cleansing, and enlightening the streets of the town, whereby every inhabitant who had property of a certain value should have full power to purchase lamps, and to appoint people from time to time to repair, clean and light the streets. This was part of an attempt to raise Birmingham's status from a vast, struggling village, to that of a noble city, and to clear a large area of wretchedness from times past.

Like all projects, however beneficial, which involve the expenditure of public money, the Lamp Act met with opposition from those who seemed to prefer darkness and mire without tax, to cleanliness, light and wider streets with eight pence in the pound to pay. One person expressed himself in the local journal in favour of a voluntary subscription, rather than a compulsory rate, hoping no doubt to enjoy the benefits without contributing to the cost.

Many reasons were given for improving conditions:- robbery for example, was seen as the work of darkness, so to introduce light would help to protect property. Also, many unfortunate accidents would be presented - 70,000 people were now using streets once used by 7,000 and in similar condition; this was particulary dangerous to women, children and those of feeble age.

The opposition was unsuccessful. On the 24th April, the "Gazette" announced that the Act had been passed by the House of Commons on the previous Friday with only one vote against. The final stage was reached early in May and the first act of parliament for the improvement of the town became law.

THE FIRST HISTORY OF BIRMINGHAM

An event of interest to every inhabitant of Birmingham must have been the publication of the first history of the town – "a history which not withstanding its shortcomings, its errors of omission and commission", was still a book which was respected.
This was Hutton's first literary work and he had begun to collect material for it as early as 1775. He spent nine months on his labour of love. He wrote:- "fearing my ability, I wrote with dread". He produced seventy five copies, the profit upon which amounted to about £40. To venture into the world as an author, without having had a previous education, was a daring attempt. The book which appeared on March 22nd, 1982, despite bearing the date of 1781 on its title page, was entitled "An History of Birmingham, to the End of the Year 1780". The volume consisted of 292 pages and the illustrations were engraved by R.Hancock, a very celebrated engraver of that period.

JOHN HOWARD'S VISIT TO BIRMINGHAM PRISON

In the 1880s, a country gentleman who was High Sheriff of the County of Bedford, was led to inquire into the treatment of prisoners, and the condition of the prisons, in his county. One was the famous "Den" which was a damp, noisy place whose foundations were in a slimy bed of the river Ouse. The wretched state of affairs revealed stirred his generous spirit, and he resolved to undertake a crusade against these filthy, disgusting dens, and against the cruel treatment to which the prisoners were often to subject.

In order to fit himself for the work, he resolved to visit gaols throughout the whole of England. The condition in which he found the Birmingham prison will be best told in his own words:-

"The gaol for this large, populous town, is called the Dungeon. The court is only about 25ft sq. Keeper's House is the front, and under it is two cells down seven steps; the straw is on bedsteads. On one side of the court two night-rooms for women, 8ft.by 5ft.9 ins, and some rooms over them; on the other side is the gaoler's stable, and one small day-room for men and women; no window. Above is a free ward for court of conscience debtors, who are cleared in forty days: this is a sizeable room, but has only one window 18ins.sq. Over it an other room, or two.

In this small court, besides the litter from the stable, there was a stagnant puddle near the sink for the gaoler's ducks. The whole prison is very offensive. At some particular times here are great numbers confined. Once in the winter of 1775, there were above 150, who had a supply of food broth, etc".

The humane inquirer again visited the gaol in 1788, and gives the following additions:-

"The court is now paved with broad stones, but dirty with fowl. There is only one day room for both sexes, over the door of which is imprudently painted, "Universal Academy".

The prison philanthropist also visited the old gaol of the parish of Aston, situated in High Street, Bordesley. Here he found: "Two damp dungeons down ten steps, and two rooms over them. Court not secure. No water.

Gaoler no salary – he keeps an ale house".

PRESS GANGS

The influence of the disasterous war with America during the 1780s was felt in Birmingham as well as elsewhere. The press gang - the system which wrought a good deal of suffering on England - was rife everywhere. On August 25th. 1777, the following paragraph in the local "Gazette" must have caused considerable terror and excitement in peoples homes:-
"The press is now very warm here and in the Neighbourhood. We hear a Gang is stationed at Gloucester, but they procure so few men that the expense is esteemed at no less than £50 a man to Government".
In Birmingham, the Warwickshire Regiment was set up as a volunteer force. They marched through the town encouraging volunteers to enlist. They were preceded by a blue flag, a band of martial music, a large piece of roast beef, several loaves of bread, and a barrel of beer. In the course of the week, several promising young men offered themselves and were enlisted.

MURDER IN THE TOWN

Several recruiting parties of soldiers were in the town in November, 1780 - among them a young man named Thomas Pitmore, a native of Cheshire who, having recklessly squandered a small fortune of about £700, had enlisted in the 2nd Regiment of foot, and was at the time a corporal.
There was also, belonging to the 36th Regiment, a young drummer, John Hammond, an American by birth. They had struck up an acquaintance and procured a brace of pistols. They then endeavoured to while away the tedium of their enforced stay in the town by playing at highway robbery.

During one of these midnight expeditions on the Coleshill Road, they met three Birmingham butchers – Schofield, Barwick and Rose, who were returning from Rugby fair and rode closely behind each other. One of the robbers attempted to seize the bridle of the first, but the horse, being young, started out of the road and ran away. Hammond then attacked the second, Wilfred Barwick, crying "Stop your horse". At the same time, he discharged a pistol at the unfortunate Barwick, who immediately fell dead. Both the robbers then retreated; the younger, who had fired the fatal shot, hid in Ward End field and was soon captured by a fourth butcher, Rann, and taken to Birmingham.

The culprit at once impeached his elder companion, and both were lodged that night in the dungeon. They were tried on March 31st, 1781, and on 2nd April were executed and hung in chains at Washwood Heath.

THE POST

Prior to 1784, the mail of the whole of the country was conveyed by postbags on horse back, at an average rate, including stoppages of these to three or four miles an hour, but in that year, one of the greatest reforms ever made in The Post Office was effected by the introduction of the plan of John Palmer, by which these important despatches were conveyed by stage-coaches which were henceforth designated as mail-coaches.

In 1783, the postal service was described as "Instead of being the swiftest is almost the slowest conveyance in the country; and though, from the great improvement in our roads, other carriers have mended their speed, the post as slow as ever. It is likewise very unsafe, as the frequent robberies of it testify; and to avoid a loss of this nature people generally cut bank bills or bills at sight in two, and send the bills by different posts. The mails are generally entrusted to some idle boy, without character, on a worn out hack, and who, so far from being able to defend himself or escape from a robber, is more likely to be in league with him."

The first mails were conveyed to Birmingham by the new mode on 23rd August, 1785.

A TOWN REJOICING

In early November, 1788, the townsmen were preparing to celebrate the centenary of the glorious revolution of 1688. The principal inhabitants were to dine together at the Hotel, and illuminations, bonfires, and other popular manifestations of joy were intended. However, on the day before, a notice was issued:-

"... no Illuminations, Bonfires or Fireworks will take place on the Celebration of the Revolution Jubilee and Gunpowder Plot".

A Dr Langford from the "Gazette" reported the celebrations despite the threatened prosecutions:-

"At night the principal streets of the town were illuminated. There were fireworks, they rang out merry peal, and the assembly at the Hotel was more numerous and respectable than any ever known in the town... and the majority of the guests were appropriately dressed in blue coats, with orange capes, emblematical buttons, and silver medals. An appropriate ode, set to music, was performed at the dinner."

The next year saw the town rejoicing over the happy recovery of the King from that illness which threatened to incapacitate him from any further part in the affairs of the realm. Already a proposal had been made to transfer to the Prince of Wales and Birmingham had loyally expressed her adherance to the Regent elect; but by the end of February, more hopeful news came of the state of the King's health, and as soon as certain intelligence as to his well-being was received, the inhabitants furnished their windows with lights, and rung the bells of the churches.

The streets were thronged, despite inclement weather. A huge bonfire, at which 3 tons of coal were consumed, was kindled in front of the Navigation Office, fireworks were displayed in various parts of the town, and at Soho the manufactory, house, and grounds, of Mr Boulton were "completely and grandly" illuminated with many thousand lamps of various colours.

On the appointed day of public Thanksgiving for the King's recovery, a townsman gratified the people, by letting off from St Paul's Square, a Mongolfier balloon of 50 feet in circumference, which glided over the town. The local laureate, Collins, celebrated with a poem; services were held; a special form of prayer and psalms composed for the occasion, were read and sung at the Jews' synagogue; and everybody, both rich and poor joined in expressing joy that the good and kindhearted "Farmer George" was able to preside over his people again.

THE BIRMINGHAM LIBRARY

In 1779, the townsmen decided to found a Library, later known as the "Old Library". Early records of this institution and its founders are lost. The first home of library was in Snow Hill, where it was open only for one hour each morning for the delivery and return of books. Each member paid a guinea entrance and six shillings per annum and "their number was so small, that they could scarcely have quarrelled had they been inclined, and their whole stock might have been laid in a handkerchief". The entire collection of books was

originally kept in a small old-fashioned "corner cupboard".
By 1782, the library contained nearly 500 volumes. In 1783, the question of novel reading occupied the attention of the commitee who oversaw the work of the library. By 1786, the library had grown to 1,600 volumes and the annual subscription was now a guinea and a half.
In 1787, there arose a fierce and bitter dispute as to the non-admission of works of theological controversy.
After much debate and motions, controversial divinity was excluded from the library. It was also resolved "that those Subscribers who live one mile from the Town be allowed one extra day for the return of a book, and those who live at the distance of two miles be allowed two days extra". It was also resolved that the hours of the librarian's attendance be from three o'clock to six in the afternoon between September and May and from three until eight from May to September. In time, the library expanded, sought temporary premises and was later rebuilt.

BIRMINGHAM IN 1790

Extracts of narrative:-
"Starting from Camp Hill, as we pass the end of Coventry Road, we enter the domain of brick and timber. The old gaol of Aston attracts notice, with its grim-looking irons hanging outside, and the old-fashioned, bulk-windowed alehouse in front, kept by the gaoler. The half-timbered houses are now becoming fewer, but there are still a few remaining to give picturesequences to the old "street called Dirtey".
The Chapel of St John the Baptist, with its heavy square tower does not harmonise ill with the quaint

ILLUS:- OLD SMITHY AND OPEN FORGE IN
        DIGBETH.

surroundings, now that the newness of its red brick has been toned down by the smoke; and the entrance to the town may still be said to be through a "pretty street".

Reaching the banks of the Rea, in Deritend, the first noticeable improvement is the erection of a new bridge over the stream. In early times, before the water was dammed up to supply Cooper's Mill, the stream was shallow enough to be crossed by stepping stone, then several paltry bridges were erected, which were barred, chained and locked and had an attendant bar-keeper. These rude wooden bridges were easily washed away by winter floods.

As we pass along Digbeth, many of the old gabled, half-timbered houses have given way to newer buildings and many of the smithies with their quaint old shops have gone. One remained - John Roberts - whose health the smoke of the town and the lack of an "improved dwelling" had failed to injure and who lived to a hundred and three years.

(John Roberts was an extraordinary man who retained his faculties to the last, and married three wives, by whom he had 28 children - he was nearly 80 when he married his last wife and had six of the children by her).

"Another of the quaint and picturesque old houses which escaped the ravages of the time is that known as the " Old Digbeth Tripe House".

At St Martin's Church, considerable alterations have been made. In 1781, the spire was found to be a decayed and exceedingly unsafe condition, and had to be replaced and rebuilt. Alterations took place inside the church, which included new pews.

"Passing further up the High Street, we notice the most improvement yet effected under the Lamp Acts - The opening of the end of New Street. The old houses blocking up the of the street (later to become a

ILLUS:- "OLD TRIPE HOUSE IN DIGBETH".

principal thoroughfare) are now removed and we no longer pass under a narrow gateway to reach it. The Welsh Cross still stands and the Beast Market still hinders the traffic in Dale End. The horse-fair has been removed to what was Bricklin Lane, near the end of Smallbrook Street. As we pass along Coleshill Street, we come upon an entirely new suburb. The fair estate of Dr Ash has already begun to be built upon, and is cut up into broad, well made streets. The doctor's house is undergoing considerable internal attention, and the building will be ready for opening as a Chapel of the Establishment before the end of 1791.

While these changes were taking place on the one side of the town, the last vestiges were being removed of an old estate on the other.

The pleasant, park-like estate of the Colmore family and New Hall passed away to become one of the grimiest districts. We cross the estate, and reach the foot by Snow Hill. On the crest of the hill beyond, we leave the buildings behind us, and obtain a delightful view over the valley - across to the right towards Aston, where, behind the lofty trees in the park, we discern the graceful spire of the church, and the minarets of the old hall of the Holtes; and beyond these we get a view of Barr Beacon."

In the valley to the left of this was a mysterious building with a story. An ingenious mechanic, Richard Ford by name, noticing his friends spending money at the alehouse, decided to set aside two shillings a day to build for himself a picturesque dwelling on a piece of waste, boggy land at Hockley, by using the slag that lay round the nearby Aston furnace as building material. With his horse and cart, he would carry the slag until he had enough to erect his building.

In front of the house was the date of 1473 in small pebble stones, but the real date was probably about 1780. When overgrown with ivy, it presented a

ILLUS:- OLD BUILDING CALLED "HOCKLEY
        ABBEY".

picturesque appearance.

"Returning to the town we visit next the charming, breezey site of the intended Crescent, commanding a view of the pleasant district surrounding St Paul's, little built upon. Away to the left rising in the distance, and directly before us a view over fields and gardens to the Summer Hill estate, the prospect of being bounded by the Icknield Street, lined on either side by a row of pleasant shady trees.
Passing from the pleasant site of the Crescent, we come to the road leading to the Five Ways, which afterwards became Broad Street, but was merely a foot-way, along which there were scarcely half-a-dozen houses. At the Five Ways, a little village had sprung up, and so the handsome modern thoroughfare leading to Birmingham's most beautiful suburb was commenced at the end farthest from the town. About half way between the Five Ways and the town was an enclosed piece of land used as the Jew's Burial Ground".

WILLIAM MURDOCH

The Soho foundary really started to grow in importance in 1775 when Boulton decided to go ahead with the manufacture of steam engines. One of the greatest difficulties experienced by the Soho firm was that of obtaining skilled workmen; another was that of keeping them when they had obtained them. The first difficulty they overcame by confining the men to special classes of work, carrying the division of labour to the farthest possible point; by continued practice in the same narrow groove, the men acquired considerable proficiency in their special department of work. The second difficulty was one which required all the tact and spirit of Matthew Boulton to cope with it.

ILLUS:- MATTHEW BOULTON.

There were tempters from abroad continually lurking about Soho, offering heavy bribes to obtain access to the works; and still heavier to lure away skilled workmen. The "Waggon and Horses" Inn, at Handsworth, was a hot-bed of temptation for gathering intelligence about the secrets of Soho. It was here that Pickard picked up the idea of the crank steam engine, and thus forestalled Watt in the use of that improvement.

Boulton was fortunate enough to meet with the one person who gave promise of becoming a thoroughly trustworthy workman and valuable helper – a young Scotsman, William Murdoch, who had travelled to England in search of employment.

William called at Soho in 1777, to ask for a job and he saw Boulton – work was slack with them, and every place was filled. William nervously kept twirling his hat with his hands. It was not a felt hat, nor a cloth hat, but painted and composed of some unusual material. The hat was made of wood – William had turned it himself on a lathe. Boulton saw the young man with new interest and estimation – his wooden hat was proof that he was a mechanic of no mean skill, and he was asked to call again.

When he next called, he was put upon a trial job, which gained him a permanent situation, at fifteen shillings per week. Murdoch soon proved himself worthy of confidence and was sent to Cornwall where many Boulton engines were at work in draining the mines, and had hitherto required the almost constant presence of James Watt.

While living in Cornwall as resident engineer, Murdoch turned his attention to the subject of the locomotive engine, and actually brought the idea to a certain degree of perfection – this later fell into oblivion until George Stephenson took it in hand, and carried the project to a successful issue.

When Murdoch returned to Soho, he was given the general supervision and management of the mechanical department, where he introduced several valuable improvements in the manufacture of the steam engine. But the invention by which his name will chiefly be remembered was that of lighting by gas. The inflammable qualities of coal gas had long been known, but William Murdoch applied the knowledge to practical uses. He turned his attention to the subject and dreamed of the brilliant artificial light of the future.

He put his discovery of the production of gas from coal to use, by lighting his offices with gas and his house at Redruth. He also made a portable gas lantern. With this he lighted his way home at night, across the moors to Redruth.

APPEARANCE OF THE TOWN AT THE BEGINNING OF THE 19TH CENTURY

Towards the upper end of New Street, was the Old Post Office - a quiet, unpretentious looking private house, with a small one-storey room adjoining, over which could be seen a glimpse of St Philip's Church, picturesquely surrounded with trees. To this place came, daily, the mail coaches from all parts of the country.

Where Bennett's Hill enters New Street was once covered with yellow corn where sun-browned children would romp and gather ripe blackberries. This later became the legal and insurance centre.

Early in the 19th century, a structure was erected in the Bull Ring, which provoked considerable criticism and ridicule - the Egyptian Conduit, commonly known as "Pratchett's Folly". This was supposed to be a significant improvement upon the more humble pump and was erected by Mr R.Pratchett in 1807. The old houses around the St Martin's Church were removed, and it was by their removal that the old pump was left prominently conspicuous. A description of these houses was given from the personal recollections of an old lady in 1866:-

"At the corner opposite Digbeth, there were two flights of steps, and at the top of the first flight was a house occupied by the beadle of the church, who was a firework maker, named Neale, and used to make the fireworks for Old Vauxhall, which was then a fashionable place of the resort and amusement. Coming to the bottom again towards the Bull Ring, the first shop was a saddler's named Bassett; the next, at the corner, Taylor's, a grocer; while Wright, a combmaker, and Probin, an auctioneer and broker, occupied the next two shops. The well-known printer and bookseller, Belcher, lived at the next house, and his immediate neighbour was Ashmore, who kept a china and earthernware shop. Taverner's shop was next, followed by what we now call a slop shop. I remember that wagoners' frocks were among the principal articles of the trade at that time. Next to this shop was Mr Hall's, a watchmaker, while Cotton's shop completed the row in this direction".

The same article gave the same idea of the names in the locality. The Red Lion was an old inn which had stood since the end of the 16th century; in a cellar-house occupied by a quack doctor, named Poole, was The Pump from which the famous "Digbeth Water" was taken and hawked round the town in carts, for sale. Two doors below that was the well-known White Hart Inn, from whence the Plague started. On the other side of Digbeth, almost opposite the house which contained the "Digbeth Water" was another equally well known "Cock Pump". A ballard was once written called "The Cock Pump's Complaint" in which the neglected pump called upon the authorities to put him in repair and to

ILLUS:- OLD VIEW OF THE MOAT, FROM LOWER
END OF MOAT END.

make him decent.

Bradford Street was very narrow and there was a small house at the top, nearly round the in shape. Here a very remarkable-looking old woman used to live. People said she had sold her body to the doctors, so that they might dissect her when she was dead. She sold sucks and sweets and children were delighted to spend their money there, in order to see her.

19TH CENTURY AMUSEMENTS

Alongside cock-fighting, badger-drawing and bear baiting were some more refined and humane amusements.

For those of the working classes who cared for the pastime of gardening, there were little allotments called "guinea gardens" encircling the town on every side – little plots of ground, let for a guinea a year, laid out with flowers, or planted with vegetables, currant and gooseberry bushes, and strawberries. These "guinea gardens" afforded a pleasant retreat where the weary artisan might breathe the pure country air after toiling all day in the close surroundings of the factory or the workshop. Gradually, they were enveloped.

The first decade of the nineteenth century saw the local theatre increasingly popular. It played host to a number of serious plays and pantomimes.

The miscellaneous entertainments of this period were such as were common in all great towns: a panorama in New Street, Waxworks in High Street, "the invisible lady" at the hotel in the Temple Row, the "Pandeau Band" and "the Pantagonian Sampson" at the Shakespeare. There was an ampitheatre, at the back of the Stork, in 1802. Our old townsfolk could not have suffered for the lack of pleasure at this time.

TWO DISTINGUISHED VISITORS

The town, as it increased in influence and nobility, began to attract people of note. Among the most distinguished of the visitors was Lord Nelson. On Monday, August 30th, 1802, the hero of the Nile, accompanied by Lady Hamilton and others, arrived at Style's (later the Royal) hotel.

Thousands of inhabitants went out to meet him that afternoon and crowded round the hotel, shouting their rough welcomes, while the bells clanged peals, and Nelson stood at the windows for hours to satisfy their curiosity. In the evening, the party visited the Theatre. The hardy Birmingham men took the horses from the hero's carriage and dragged it in disorderly but triumphant procession to the play. The whole house rose at him as he entered, and offered him a rare ovation. On his return, at midnight, men with torches lined the streets and he was drawn back to his hotel.

He walked to the manufactory of Mr Clay in Newhall Street, the sword manufactory of Messrs. Woolley and Deakin, Edmund Street; the button establishment of Messrs. Smith; the buckle and ring manufactory of Messrs. Simcox and Timmins, Livery Street; and the patent sash manufactory of Messrs. Timmins and Jordan, St Paul's Square and when he stepped into his carriage to proceed to the famous stained glass manufactory of Mr Eginton, at Handsworth, the horses were unharnessed by the crowd, who drew him there with their hands and where he was received by a large party of young ladies who in white robes, strewed flowers before him on his path.

Soho was also seen, where appropriate medals were struck, and where an interview was had with Matthew Boulton in his bed-room. In the evening, there was a grand banquet, to which Nelson was invited. There, Lady Hamilton sang several charming songs. Nelson left the following day.

In May, 1805, HRH Prince William of Gloucester stopped on his way Liverpool. The Loyal Birmingham Volunteers and a party of Royal Dragoons greeted him at Camp Hill and accompanied him to the hotel. The Prince inspected them and was conducted to the principal places of interest in the town.

LOCAL ENTERPRISE - GUNS AND JEWELLERY

There exists a popular error among those who know the town little,with Birmingham as "grimy with the dense smoke of furnaces, echoing with the clang of forges, gleaming with great fires, and busy in the production of iron". No picture of the town could be wider of the mark. Scarcely a bar or a pig has been smelted with in its boundaries, but there was a solitary furnace at Aston until the end of the 18th century. The blast was blown by a water wheel, and one of the first steam engines in this neighbourhood was erected to supply it. Aston Furnace was itself blown out shortly before 1795, and from that period the iron-smelting was driven away from the town into the district popularly known as "The Black Country".

The American War in 1775 gave a considerable stimulus to the Birmingham gun trade, bringing in a succession of large orders, and these had scarcely been completed when the French War commenced; the total supply of arms to the Government from Birmingham during this period has been estimated at not less than half a million. Birmingham also supplied fire-arms to the Irish Ordnance department, for use by the military and yeomanry, called into existence by the rebellion; the various companies of Legal Volunteers throughout England and Scotland, and to the East Indian Company, besides those for private use. Altogether, the

Birmingham gun-makers must have turned out at least 750,000 stand of arms between 1775 and the close of the eighteenth century.

Jewellery was a comparatively small trade in those days.The jewellers themselves were not very numerous, with only about a dozen establishments in the town. There were a number of "small masters", some of whom were earning for Birmingham that unenviable reputation which rendered the outer world sceptical as to all jewellery turned out of the Midlands. Hence, the old saying: "Give a Birmingham maker a guinea and a copper kettle and he'll make you a hundred pounds worth of jewellery". It was not all undeserved, the odium which was cast upon "Brummagen" trinkets. One ingenious individual cut and polished some cinders from the calx of Aston furnaces set them in rings and brooches, and sold them as fragments of Pompey's Pillar. The profuse use of gold and silver in various manufactures, in ornamentation, gilding, etc, brought into existence a new and lucrative occupation. Prior to 1758, the sweepings of workshops (containing minute fragments of these precious metals), were thrown into the streets, or cast off as an incumbrance. One man began to collect the sweepings, and would give the artisans a sort of Christmas treat in recompense.

By and by a second "golden dustman" arose and competition ensued as to which should give the most sumptuous treat; quarrels occurred occasionally among the workmen as to which of the rivals should be favoured, which attracted the attention of employers to the subject. They resolved in future to keep the refuse themselves, and found it a valuable addition to their profit. One manufacturer realised as much as £1,000 a year from this source alone. The art of refining began. But the sweepings of the earlier period, lie buried beneath the streets of Birmingham, some of which "may be literally paved with gold and silver".

COACH TRAVEL 1770 - 1820

"Flying Coaches" performed the journey from Birmingham to London in 2½ days. In the year 1770, there were probably not more than half a dozen coaches running from Birmingham. In 1820, it was estimated in an article in the "Scot's Magazine", that there were no less than 84 coaches belonging to Birmingham, of which 40 were daily. At the same time, Manchester had but 70, and Liverpool only 60.

Meanwhile the improved method of road-making introduced about this time by Mr Macadam, once more effected an appreciable increase in speed, so that between Birmingham, Liverpool and Manchester, ten miles and one furlong per hour was a realistic rate, and between the town and Sheffield, Pontefract, Leeds, London, Bath and on other roads, ten miles an hour was maintained.

Many reports have been given of the joys of coach travel - George Eliot for example in "Felix Holt" wrote in 1866 "the great roadside inns were still brilliant with well-polished tankards, the smiling glances of pretty bar-maids, and the repartees of jocose ostlers". The pleasures of the road, the delight of rattling along country roads, through old-fashioned villages and towns, through the most charming English scenery have often been recounted. But there was also a "shady" side to this picture.

It was not always bright sunshine or clear, frosty air; there were deep snows and perilous fogs to be encountered, and driving sleet and drenching rain, to be endured by the outsiders with what patience they could muster. Then there were not infrequently - especially in Birmingham, the half-way house of England - necessary changes at uncomfortable times of the night, and often in the worst of weather.

Thomas de Quincey tells such a tale :- "in my case....

I have passed through Birmingham a hundred times...
it always happened to rain, except once. As to the
noise, never did I sleep at the enormous "Hen and
Chickens"... I had a reason to complain that the
discreet hen did not gather her vagrant flock to roost
at less variable hours. Till two or three I was kept
waking by those who were retiring, and about three
commenced the morning function's of the Pater....
collecting several freights".

William Gladstone also described a similar experience:-
"My recollections of the casual hours in Birmingham
are.... less pleasant. The coach inns were bad. The
times of stopping chosen in reference to anything
rather than the comfort of the passengers. I have been
turned out of the Liverpool coach, the "Aurora" at four
o'clock on a winter's morning, sometimes in frost or
snow, and offered breakfast for which this was the only
time allowed; while the luggage was charged upon a
barrow. Behind the barrow we mournfully trudged
along the streets to the other hotel; Castle or Albion,
or Hen and Chickens, from which the sister coach was
to start for the South. The average rate of coaches
during my boyhood did not quite touch seven miles an
hour".

Within the town, hackney coaches did not find their
way into Birmingham until a hundred years after their
introduction into the metropolis – and then only in
singular number, for there was but one in the town in
1775. By the year 1819, they had increased to thirty;
and at the same period one-horse cars were first
introduced , and an attempt was made to popularise the
cab, or "two-wheeled car" as it was then called, but
being very unsafe, they were abandoned. Eleven years
later, however, there were about sixty of them, and the
old two-horse coaches, having declined in favour, were
falling into dis-use.

There were many hindrances in the way of traffic: there

were tollgates at every outlet towards the country; the streets were ill-made and beset with dangers, in the numerous holes and ruts and rubbish heaps, and with numerous obstructions from the old-established outdoor markets for pigs, cattle, and agricultural produce.

In 1806, some attempt was made to govern behaviour on the road: carts were to give way to coaches, no person was to ride or lead a horse or wheel a barrow, on the footpaths; and a drunken driver was to be fined five shillings, and for profane swearing one, two or five shillings.

"The rule of the road is a paradox quite
As you drive, ride, or walk it along,
If you go to the left, you are sure to go right
But if you go to the right you are wrong".

There was also a rule for pedestrians:-

"Pass left to left the passing throng
for right to right is doubly wrong".

PINFOLD STREET SCHOOL

On the site of the old Dungeon was built a national school. It was erected in 1813, by public subscription, and was calculated to accomodate nearly 1,000 children. One of the most frequent visitors to the school was the Rev Dr Hook, a Lecturer at St Philip's Church.

"The doctor was a great enthusiast on the question of education and when he had thoroughly drilled the first class he used to empty his pockets of all the silver he had, telling the master to get change, and then to divide it among the lads. Sometimes, it would amount to twopence each – when school broke up, there was a scamper to "Lease Lane" where a very clean old woman sold "hot suck" a sweetmeat much loved by the juveniles then. For some reason or other, the scholars

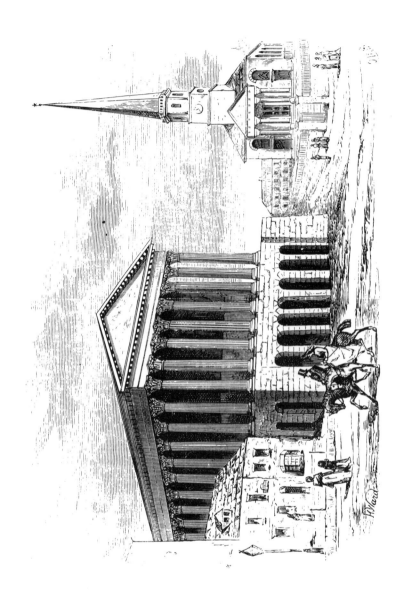

ILLUS:- THE TOWN HALL.

of Pinfold Street School had acquired the nickname of the "drowned bulldogs" and many a fight was had over that unpleasant epithet. School fights between this and several other schools acquired such importance that the shopkeepers in the town began to put up their shutters, till the presence of the redoubtable 'Billy Hall' with his ash plant, put terror into the heels of the combatants, and soon cleared the streets.

I CAN'T FIND BRUMMAGEN - A BRUMMIE'S LAMENT

Full twenty years, and more, are past
Since I left Brummagen,
But I set out for home at last,
To good old Brummagen.
But every place is altered so,
There's hardly a single place I know;
And it fills my heart with grief and woe,
For I can't find Brummagen..

As I walked down our street,
As used to be in Brummagen,
I know'd nobody I did meet;
They change their faces in Brummagen.
Poor old Spiceal Street's half gone,
And the poor Old Church stands all alone,
And poor old I stand here to groan,
For I can't find Brummagen.

But 'mongst the changes we have got,
In good old Brummagen,
They've made a market of the Mott (Moat),
To sell the pigs in Brummagen.
But what has brought us most ill luck,
They've filled up poor old Pudding Brook,

Where in the mud I've often stuck
Catching jackbanils (sticklebacks) near Brummagen.

But what's more melancholy still
For poor old Brummagen,
They've taken away all Newhall-hill
Poor old Brummagen!
As Easter time, girls fair and brown,
Used to come rolly-polly down,
And show'd their legs to half the town,
Oh! the good old sights in Brummagen.

Down Peck Lane I walked alone,
To find out Brummagen,
There was a dungil (dungeon) down and gone!
What no rogues in Brummagen?
They've taken it to the street called Moor,
A sign that rogues they get no fewer,
The rogues won't like to go there I'm sure,
While Peck Lane's in Brummagen.

I remember one John Growse,
A bucklemaker in Brummagen:
He built himself a country house,
To be out of the smoke of Brummagen:
But though John's country house stands still,
The town itself has walked up hill,
Now he lives beside of a smoky mill,
In the middle of the streets of Brummagen.

Amongst the changes that abound,
In good old Brummagen,
May trade and happiness be found,
In good old Brummagen;
And tho' no Newhall-hill we've got,
Nor Pudding Brook, nor any Mott,
May we always have enough to boil the pot,

In good old Brummagen.

This was sung to the tune of the air "Rob Ray McGregor O"!

CANNON HILL AND OTHER PARKS

On 1st September, 1873, the town was enriched by the acquisition of a noble park in the neighbourhood of Moseley, the gift of Miss Ryland, of Bakford Hill, Warwick. The donor modestly declined to allow the park to be called after her own name, as the Council unanimously wished to do, and it bore simply the name of the old estate out of which it was formed, Cannon Hill Park. At the request of Miss Ryland, the park was opened without any public ceremony. The Council, with the Mayor, came to the park, and simply declared it open for the use of the people. To every visitor on that day was presented, as a memento, an inscribed card.
The park was 57 acres in extent bordered by the river Rea, Moseley Road, Pershore Road, and Edgbaston Road which housed the principal entrance. It was described by its curator, Mr Rodway in his "Handbook":-
"The ground is beautifully undulating, is well wooded and was laid out with great taste. Several acres are devoted to ornamental gardening, including shrubberies, in which are planted many choice and rare evergreens. The natural attractions have been very much enhanced by the formation of large pools, which are surrounded by plantations and pleasant walks. Swans, Canadian geese, ducks, and other water fowl, are kept on these pools, which are also used for boating, a small charge being made for the lessee of the pools for the use of the boats. Near the boat-house are landing stages. The bathing pool is 216ft by 100ft, with

a depth varying from 2ft 6in to 5ft 6in. The bottom is concrete, and the water is kept fresh and pure by a small stream passing through it.....".

A number of other parks followed. On 25th May, 1875, the Council decided to purchase, for the sum of £5,390, a piece of waste land (eight acres in extent) near the Moseley Road, called Hollier's Charity Land, and to convert the same into a public park. It was at first intended to be called Camp Hill Park, but this sounded to similar to Cannon Hill and changed to Highgate Park. The new park was opened on June 2nd, 1876, by the Major, Joseph Chamberlain. No one who had before crossed the dismal piece of land, crowded with the brick-ends and other unsightly refuse would have readily identified with the exquisite little park, with its broad terrace and winding walks, its shrubberies and bright parterres, and its smooth trim lawns. The lower end, near Alcester Street, was paved with asphalte and served admirably as a playground for local juveniles.

On the day of the inauguration of Highgate Park, another gift was announced by Miss Ryland, of about 43 acres of land for a new Park at Small Heath. Four days later, the Council decided upon the purchase of yet another park – the Summerfield estate situated between Dudley Road and Icknield Park Road, Winson Green, for £9,000. This was twelve acres in extent and contained some fine old trees.

The major Birmingham parks were as follows:-

	Size	Opened
Adderley Park	10 acres	1856
Calthorpe Park	31 acres	1857
Aston Park	50 acres	1858
Cannon Hill Park	57 acres	1873
Highgate Park	8 acres	1876
Summerfield Park	12 acres	1876

Burbury Street Recreation Ground   4 acres   1877
Small Heath Park   41 acres   1879
This meant that the people of Birmingham possessed
over 200 acres of parks and playgrounds by 1879.

THE ELEMENTARY EDUCATION ACT, 1870

The Elementary Education Act was speedily adopted in
Birmingham with the first School Board for the town
taking place in November of that year. By 1879, the
Board had opened 24 schools, all of them
architecturally considered, ornaments of the town. The
following is a list of these schools with the date of
opening, and the number of scholars for whom
accomodation is provided including boys, girls, and
infants:-

Name of School	Date of Opening	No.of Children
1.Farm Street	July, 1873	1055
2.Bloomsbury	March, 1873	1059
3.Jenkins Street	May, 1873	1136
4.Steward Street	July, 1873	1055
5.Garrison Lane	July, 1873	967
6.Elkington Street	May, 1874	983
7.Lower Windsor Street	November, 1874	1055
8.Allcock Street	April, 1875	1052
9.Rea Street South	July, 1875	1070
10.Osler Street	November, 1875	1025
11.Dartmouth Street	May-Oct, 1876	1053
12.Smith Street	June, 1876	972
13.Bristol Street	October, 1876	1023
14.Nelson Street	November, 1876	971
15.Norton Street	November, 1876	994
16.Moseley Road	January, 1877	1017

17.Fox Street	January, 1877	1017
18.Brookfields	November, 1877	1018
19.Summer Lane	September, 1877	1352
20.Oozells Street	January, 1879	807
21.Dudley Road	June, 1878	1220
22.Little Green Lane	August, 1878	1347
23.Hutton Street	January, 1879	1095
24.Montgomery Street	July, 1879	1000

The total amount spent in the erection of school-buildings and purchase of sites, is £349,575 19s 1d the total cost of school maintenance for eight years was £94,928.

"BARONESS" VON BECK

In 1851, an incident occured which led to a great deal of censure and an outburst of indignation. A lady, known as "the Baroness Von Beck" came to Birmingham and passed herself off as a Hungarian exile and rendered good service to the cause of independence. She had previously published a book and visited the principal towns in England, to obtain subscribers for her new book.

Many of the Liberal leaders in Birmingham assisted her, and as she fell ill during her stay in the town, she was invited to stay at the house of a Mr Tyndall, where she was treated with great kindness and consideration. Subsequently, it transpired that the "Baroness" was an impostor, and was suspected moreover, of being a spy, in the pay of the Austrian Government. Her real name was Wilhemina Racidula and she was a woman of indifferent reputation. She was arrested and conveyed to the Moor Street prison.

On 30th August, the case came before the magistrates, but while the "Baroness" was being led from her cell to the dock, she died in the ante-room of the court.

DICKENS VISITS BIRMINGHAM

Christmas, 1853, readings were given by Mr Dickens in the Town Hall. On 27th December, he read the "Christmas Carol" and on 29th "The Cricket on the Heath". On 30th, when at his special desire the price of admission was reduced to sixpence in order to afford the working classes the opportunity of being present, he repeated the "Carol". This was in reality the first appearance of Charles Dickens as a reader before any large audience. However he first tested his skills before a less intelligent and exacting audience at the dull little Cathedral city of Peterborough. He said:-
"Here was an opportunity for testing the matter without risk; an antidiluvian country town, an audience of farmers' sons and daughters, rural shop-keepers, and a few parsons". One who was present at his first reading of the immortal "Carol" wrote:-
"As the clock struck the appointed hour, a red, jovial face, unrelieved by the heavy moustache which the novelist has since assumed, a broad, high forehead and a perfectly Micawber-like expanse of shirt-collar and front appeared above the red baize box, and a full, sonorous voice rang out the words "Marley-was-dead-to-begin-with".... The voice held all spell-bound. Its depth of quiet feeling when the ghost of past Christmasses led the dreamer through the long-forgotten scenes of boyhood - it's embodiment of burly good nature when old Fezziwig's calves were twinkling in the dance - its tearful suggestiveness when the spirit of Christmasses to come pointed to the nettle-grown, neglected grave of the unloved man - its exquisite pathos by the death-bed of Tiny Tim, dwell yet in memory like a long-known tune. That one night's

reading in the quaint little city, so curiously brought about, so ludicrous almost in its surroundings, committed Mr Dickens to the career of a public reader; and he had since derived nearly as large an income from his readings as from the copyright of his novels. Charles Dickens received monies amounting to £227 19s 9d, plus gifts and hospitality for himself, his wife and his son, for his three readings.

THE WOMEN'S HOSPITAL

In 1871, a hospital was founded for the reception and treatment of Women "afflicted with diseases peculiar to their sex". It consisted of an out and in-patient free and paying department. All women whose average weekly family earnings do not exceed 40s were at once admitted. The hospital was originally in the Cresent but in 1878, the In-patient Dept was removed to move to more convenient premises at Sparkhill. Once again Miss Ryland, a local benefactor, stepped in with money towards the alterations.

BIRMINGHAM 1841 - 1879

Since 1832, the entire appearance changed considerably. Many of the old narrow streets were swept away; a group of narrow streets and lanes were removed to make way for the site of the central railway station, and others followed in the clearing of the site of the Snow Hill Station. The station was rebuilt in 1870 and became a light and elegant building worthy of the Great Western Company. On its completion, the old buildings in Little Charles Street and Edmund Street were removed and the line of Edmund Street was altered and continued.

The Old Inkleys were, for the most part, removed and many of the old buildings in Moor Street, and on the site of Albert Street. A portion of the new street undertaken by the Town Council, called Corporation Street, was laid out and built upon. The old line of Ann Street and Colmore Row was altered, and the whole of the north side rebuilt, forming one of the finest thoroughfares in the town. Two large hotels and other public buildings were erected and the line finished by the Council House, a structure which rose to 162 feet and measured 296 feet in length.

The Post Office was twice moved. First, from the corner of Bennett's Hill to the building formerly known as the New Royal Hotel and again in 1874, to the new building erected for the purpose opposite the Town Hall. The old building was then taken down, and with it passed away one of the old-fashioned suburban mansions of New Street, "Portugal House", which was built by the once celebrated "Beau Green".

Great attention was paid to the paving of the streets; nearly all footways were paved either with flags or blue bricks, and the old-fashioned "petrified kidneys" had mainly been abolished. The roadways in the principal streets were paved with wood, and in many others with granite blocks. The thick, black, greasy mud with which the streets used to be flooded during the winter was by this time largely unknown.

Open spaces were improved by the planting of shrubs and flowers. The old pleasant suburbs, as they were in 1832, had grown into thickly populated districts. The old suburbs such as Aston, Ashted, Bloomsbury, Nechells and Balsall Heath became small towns, and the suburban residents found new houses further from the town: Acock's Green, King's Heath, Moseley, King's Norton, Harborne, Perry Barr, Erdington and even as far as Sutton Coldfield. At Aston and Handsworth, the Free Libraries' Act was adopted. At Handsworth, a handsome building was erected from the designs of Messrs. Alexander and Hennian.

Aston Parish Church was one of the most interesting of the old churches of Birmingham, containing a fine series of monuments to members of the Holte family, and several very fine altar tombs. Its main feature remained its massive tower, surmounted by a tall and graceful spire. There were also new handsome modern chapels belonging to the Baptists, Independents and Wesleyans. One of the largest of these nonconformist chapels was the Independent Chapel in Wheeler Street, Lozells. The suburb of Handsworth, with its fine old Parish Church, was at this time still pleasant.

Edgbaston was one of the few suburbs close to the town which maintained its semi-rural appearance, mainly because it was the aristocratic suburb of Birmingham, and mainly the property of the landlord, Lord Calthorpe, who exercised strict care in preventing the erection of buildings which would have destroyed its character.

Of the other suburbs, the village of Saltley had little to offer except a Training College. Small Heath was home to a Small Arms factory. At Moseley was the Independent College, and the Hall and Park, on the site of the old building destroyed by the riots of 1791. Several other houses injured in the riots were also situated in this neighbourhood. The Parish Church had an old square tower erected in the reign of Henry VIII.

JOHN FREETH

John Freeth was the son of Charles Freeth, who kept the Leicester Arms, in Bell Street. After the death of his father, he succeeded to the position of host of that establishment. His poetical faculties were not confined to the verses for feasts and social gathering. His interest in writing ballads and singing them was profitable in his public house full of customers.

Among his friends he gathered around him were eleven of his townsmen who constituted themselves into a social club with their sentiments of liberalism.

To their opponents they were nicknamed "The Twelve Apostles" and "The Jacobin Club". When one of the twelve, the well-known James Bisset, called in at a Tory house, one of the members puffed smoke into his face. Bisset had already suffered many petty annoyances and insolent remarks aimed at him, but this direct and gross insult roused his indignation, and with one blow he felled the offender to the ground. There then ensued a general mêlée, in which most of the jugs and glasses came to grief, and Bisset was forcibly ejected from the house – he was sued for breakages amounting to nearly £5 and no doubt learned his lesson.

An example of Freeth's ditties is the tale of

BIRMINGHAM ALE-TASTERS

to the tune of "How happy a State does a Miller Possess".

Of all civil officers annually chose,
There's none in the Kingdom are equal to those,
Whose duty requires little more than to rove,
And taste at their pleasure, what ENGLISHMEN love.

From Bord'sley to Hockley our Province extends,
I wish one had time to address all our friends,
Of houses all free-cost, to visit, 'tis clear,
The number is more than are days in the year.

We carry no TRUNCHEONS our power to show,
With Government matters have nothing to do,

We drink with the conman, yet rank with the best,
And like ALDERMEN live at a Low Baliff's Feast.

Our good brother OFFICERS strangers must be,
When beating our rounds to the pleasures we see,
From Office of CONSTABLE troubles ensue,
But that of a TASTER is joy the year through.

For when upon duty, as custom has taught,
We call for a TANKARD, 'tis instantly brought,
And how pleasing it is for a LANDLORD to say,
"You're welcome, kind Sir – There is nothing to pay.

We visit the MARKETS and traverse the STREETS,
Our CHIEF to assist in adjusting the weights,
And wish 'twere the practice in all kinds of sales,
To down with the STEELYARDS and up with the SCALES.

The BUTCHERS may throw out their MARROW-BONE spite,
But reason informs us 'tis nothing but right,
For JUSTICE relying on the TRUTH as her guide,
When pictur'd has always the SCALES by her side.

Fill a Bumper to the TRADE, 'tis the TASTERS request,
With plenty may BRITAIN, for ever be blest,
Were DISCORD abounds may true friendship commence,
And BIRMINGHAM "flourish a thousand years hence".

On a more serious note, Freeth wrote a more doleful poem at the close of the eighteenth century....

I MUCH the Word SCARCITY hate,
And long as I find myself able,
More Cost tho' hard Times must create,
I Plenty will have as my Table.

Against the fond Wishes of some,
Though PEACE for a while is suspended,
Depend on't that BLESSING will come,
Before the next CENTURY'S ended.

The greatest of ILLS to remove,
Away with that MONSTER - STARVATION,
For thousands can FEELINGLY prove,
They too much are plagu'd with Taxation.

My Wish correspond will with many,
That soon though the Land may be found,
"Twelve Ounces of Bread for one Penny,
And good Beef at Four-pence per Pound".

The name John Freeth will probably never appear in the roll of English poets, but then the words of the poet laureate of his day – Henry James Pye – were not particularly well thought of either. Lord Byron described Pye as "a man eminently respectable in everything but his poetry". Freeth was a rather mechanical muse, and could create a stirring ballad, fitted to a popular tune to which people could sing, whenever events required it.

THE LUNAR SOCIETY

Matthew Boulton was a man of thoroughly social disposition, and made friends wherever he went. He was a favourite with children and philosophers. When at home, he took pleasure in gathering about him persons of kindred tastes and pursuits, in order at the same time to enjoy their society, and to cultivate his nature through talking with minds of the highest culture. He formed friendships with Benjamin Franklin, Dr Small, Dr Darwin, Josiah Wedgwood, Thomas Day, Lovell Edgeworth and others equally eminent, out of which grew the famous Lunar Society.

The members met once a month, by turns at each other's houses, always at the full moon, in order that distant members might drive home by moonlight – hence the name of the Society. At these meetings, the members exchanged views upon all subjects relating to literature, science and art. Here, Murdoch, Darwin and Lovell Edgeworth talked over their pet project of steam locomotion; here Dr Preistly told of his marvellous discoveries in chemistry, kindling an enthusiasm in the minds of Boulton and Watt for the study of that science, which bore fruit in certain of the ingenious productions of Soho. It was a marvellous gathering of fine intellects. Absence from the meetings was always sorely lamented by the unfortunate "Lunatic" detained for other reasons.

Each member was at liberty to bring to bring a friend with him and among the visitors thus introduced were Sir William Herschel, Sir Joseph Banks, De Luc, Dr Camper, Dr Solander, Dr Samuel Parr, Smeaton, the engineer, and many ather men of science. The Lunar Society continued to exist for some years, but one by one the members dropped off. Dr Preistley emigrated to America: Dr Withering, Josiah Wedgwood, and Dr Darwin died before the close of the century, and

ILLUS:- WATT'S HOUSE, HARPER'S HILL.

without them, a meeting of the Lunar Society was no longer what it used to be.

GREGORY WATT

Gregory was the "favourite son" of the great inventor. He was born at Harper's Hill, Birmingham in the year 1777, a period when Soho was approaching its greatest fame.

Watt's son was impetuous, self-asserting, of quick observation, original ideas, bold in language, and with a love for science and literature shown in few men of his age. Many of his school letters from Glasgow exist. His distinguishing characteristic was practical geology, and his letters abound with the result of his observations frequently illustrated with drawings of his specimens.
In 1792, he made a tour of observation to Shipston and Stratford, the next year to Malvern, and his descriptions and illustrations in pen and ink or water-colour, as in his journeys to and from Glasgow and the Scottish Coast, as well as allusions to more complete drawings and sketches, show his zeal as a travelling observer.
In 1794, he was at Heathfield, writing of the illness of his poor sister Jessy, making verses and sketches of her pet lap dog. Poor Jessy Watt's death was felt acutely by her father and mother; she died in their arms on 6th June, 1794, when Gregory was 17.
In 1797, he showed symptoms of consumption and was sent to winter in Penzance – he travelled there from Heathfield on horseback and passed the time mainly with "the immense Colony of Wedgwoods". in 1799, he was in London, spending £15 15s on fossils.
In 1800, he was at Soho. On the 1st October, he started at 5am over the wilds of Sutton Coldfield, for

Derbyshire. He reached Lichfield in two hours, and Derby (45 miles) at 4.30 in drenching rain. From there to Matlock, Stoke and Ironbridge, where he and a friend demolished four bottles of "Old Sport", and roared a song with energy at two in the morning. In May, 1801, he journeyed with Murdock on horseback to Scotland, and in the Winter left for the Continent for his health – he was ill of fever for a fortnight in Paris. He returned to England in October 1802, in ill health. In Spring 1804, in an alarming state of health, he was taken to Bath. He moved from there to the sea at Sidmouth, and then to Exeter, where he lived only a few days, and died, at noon, on Tuesday, 16th October, 1804.

He was buried in the famous corner of Handsworth Church.

THE ROBIN HOOD SOCIETY

At the close of the 18th century, Birmingham was an important centre for intellectual as well as commercial activity – She boasted Withering and Darwin in botany: Priestley in chemistry, electricity and pneumatics; Watt in mechanics and many others involved in scientific research. The town also had a number of literary and debating societies.

On 1st April, 1774, the first meeting of a little society called "The Robin Hood Free Debating Society" was held at the Red Lion Inn (in the Bull Ring). The admission was by ticket, price sixpence, but ladies (who were allowed to take part in the debates) were admitted free.

One of its advertisements illustrates the sorts of subjects debated:– Are vice and virtue innate or acquired?

- Which merits the most admiration–

frugality in a low condition, or liberality in a high station of life?

– Which of the four cardinal virtues is the greatest?

– Will open reproof or private admonition tend most to be reformation of vice?

A new society was established shortly after with meetings held at Mrs Ashton's Coffee Room, in the Cherry Orchard. At the first meeting in May, 1774, the following subjects were debated:-

– Is a Drunkard the greater Enemy to himself or Society?

– Which is most detestable in itself, or most dangerous to mankind, Treachery in friendship, or Hypocrisy in Religion?

Which are the greatest, real or imaginary evils?

After the first year, neither Society was heard of again. The next Society to be set up was the "Society for Free Debate" which met in a large room in Needless Alley (afterwards converted into a dancing room), which discussed lofty questions like "Was Brutus justifiable in killing Caesar?" Coming at the time of the reign of terror in France, this debate so excited the public mind that the Magistrates were compelled to interfere to prevent further discussion of the subject.

THE BUILDING OF THE TOWN HALL

A design for the building was supplied by Mr Barry, and exhibited at the Royal Academy, but was not adopted by the Commissioners. A description appeared in the "Gazette":- "it seemed to consist of little more than a hexastyle portico, of a very plain character; when we come, however, to examine it we discover it to be replete with beauties, and to afford evidence of

ILLUS:- STREET SCENE WITH MAGNIFICENT
TOWN HALL BEYOND.

study, of original thought, and more than ordinary feeling". The Commissioners decided to accept the design of Messrs. Hanson and Welch and building was commenced on 27th April, 1832. Many hindrances occurred, partly because the contractors had under-estimated the cost of the work, having contracted for its completion for the sum of £18,000-£19,000, whereas the total cost was about £25,000.

The hall was an imitation Roman temple design, with forty feet high Corinthian columns.

The basement formed a promenade which could offer standing room for over 1,500 people. The structure was made of brick, faced with Anglesey marble, of which the columns and their accessories were composed. The bricks were made on the spot, of the earth taken from the foundation. A new species of machinery was also constructed to raise the framed tie-beams and principals of the roof to the top of the building, a height of 70 feet. In this operation, an accident occurred, through the hook of the pulley block breaking, by which two workmen where killed. They were interned in St Philip's churchyard, and a monument, consisting of the base of the pillar from the building, was erected to their memory by their employers and fellow workmen.

The main part of the interior consisted of one large hall – the object of the building being the accomodation of the public meetings and other large assemblies. The hall could accomodate about 4,000 people sitting, but more than double that when standing up.

In a recess at the end was the magnificent organ, constructed by Hill of London at a cost of £3,000-£4,000, with 71 draw stops, 4 sets of keys, and over 4,000 pipes. The timber alone used in construction weighed between 20 and 30 tons. The bellows, of necessity, contained about 300 square feet of surface.

ROBERT RAWLINSON'S REPORT

On the passing of the Public Health Act of 1848, an enquiry was conducted by Robert Rawlinson into the natural history of the town. He remarked that "there is a marked dryness in the air than in Liverpool or Manchester; and whereas the damp atmosphere of Lancashire is necessary to the profitable spinning of cotton-yarn, the drier atmosphere of Warwickshire, is equally advantageous to the iron manufacture, to the production of polished steel implements, and the metal-plated wares in general of Birmingham".

On commerce, Mr Rawlinson wrote:-

"The variety of trades and occupations exercised tends to a more equal and general diffusion of wealth amongst the master manufactures, and the means of acquiring it in moderation among the workpeople; there are few "millionaires" connected with the trade in or near Birmingham if we except Staffordshire iron masters; there are few who occupy the position of the "cotton lords" of Manchester, or the "merchant princes" of Liverpool".

The allotment gardens, which still lingered at Edgbaston, Bordesley, Handsworth, Moseley and along the valley of the Rea were noted with commendation, and the large number of public houses – 1,363 in all – with disfavour and concern. The crowded and neglected condition of the churchyards were commented on, and contrasted with the clean and neat condition of two recently opened cemeteries – the General Cemetery at Key Hill and the adjacent Church of England Cemetery.

He commented that "the borough of Birmingham is not so healthy as it may be, an account of unpaved streets, confined courts, open middens and cesspools, and stagnant ditches. That excess of disease may be distinctly traced to crowded lodging-houses and want

ILLUS:- INSANITARY HOUSES: NO.2 COURT JOHN
STREET. (ABOUT TO BE REMOVED
UNDER THE ARTISANS DWELLINGS ACT)

ILLUS:- NO.1 COURT, STEELHOUSE LANE. (ABOUT
TO BE REMOVED UNDER THE ARTISANS
DWELLINGS ACT)

of ventilation in confined courts, and to the want of drains generally".

Rawlinson recommended a perfect system of the street, court, yard, and house drainage, with a constant and cheap supply of pure water under pressure, laid on to every house and yard. He wanted proper drains to carry away surface water and refuse. The soil in the town was recommended as use to agricultural land by irrigation, with singular advantage to the farmer and the town.

TORTURE IN THE GAOL

The Governor of the gaol in 1853 was a Mr Austin. He reputedly maintained good order, both among officers and prisoners, without harsh measures. Such was the picture that was painted. However, an inspection to the gaol found that the governor was in the habit of inflicting on the visitors, especially those of the juvenile class, punishments not sanctioned by law, and which were unfortunate for prisoners. One of the favourite instruments of torture was the crank, which one poor prisoner was condemned to turn ten thousand times a day, in an almost nude condition. Two thousand times the poor wretch had to turn the crank before breakfast, four thousand times between breakfast and dinner, and four thousand times between dinner and supper.

Several others were punished in an even more barbarous manner, bringing to mind the regime of the inquisition more than a prison discipline of one of the liberal and enlightened communities in England, during the latter half of the nineteenth century. They were kept for several days without food, fastened to the wall by a collar which almost strangled them, and made to wear a strait-jacket. When the miserable victims fainted from exhaustion, buckets of cold water were thrown over them. There were many youths driven to suicide under this monstrous treatment.

The report aroused the indignation of the people and a Government enquiry, promised by Lord Palmerston, was eagerly awaited. The Governor of the gaol tendered his registration in August, and the enquiry commenced.

"The Times" wrote: "Birmingham Gaol was in secret the scene of doings which literally filled the public with horror" and commented upon stories "which would have been thought exagerations if found in one of the Dicken's books".

THE DEATH OF CATHERINE HUTTON

On 31st march, 1846, Catherine Hutton died at the advanced age of 90. She was the only daughter of William Hutton, born on 11th February, 1756. She wrote graphic narrative of the riots. Her life was very busy owing to her maxim never to be "one moment unemployed when it was possible to be doing something". Besides writing three novels, "Oakwood Hall", "The Miser Married" and "The Welsh Mountaineer" and editing her fathers "Life", she contributed sixty papers and short stories to various periodicals; she collected upwards of 2,000 autographs, and was a collector of prints of costumes from eleven years of age, which were arranged chronologically in eight large folio volumes. Besides all this she read extensively and made patchwork. She had "ridden in every sort of vehicle except a wagon, a cart and an omnibus", and had been "in thirty nine of the counties of England and Wales, twenty-six times at London, twenty-one at watering places on the coast, and five inland". Truly a remarkable woman of her time.

GRAND FÊTES AT ASTON HALL

In the Spring of 1856, Mr John Walsh conceived the idea of organising a grand fête at Aston Hall on behalf of the Queen's Hospital, the finances of which were at a very low ebb. When the day arrived it soon became evident that such a fête was about to be held as had not been heard of before!

Upwards of 50,000 people from Birmingham, from the Black Country and from the surrounding rural districts, poured into the usually quiet little village of Aston, which was gaily decorated for the occasion; from the belfry of the fine old village church, the bells chimed a joyous welcome.

The delighted thousands thronged throughout the park, and in and out of the quaint old corridors and noble state appartments of the Hall. Old English games, and innocent fun and pleasure of every description occupied the afternoon, and in the evening, the fête was brought to a close with a grand display of fireworks. The receipts amounted to £2,222, 12s 5sd, of which £1,500 profit was handed over to the Queen's Hospital.

There had been some jealousy on the part of certain persons that the proceeds of the fête had not been divided with the General Hospital, so Mr Walsh and his friends organized a second fête on behalf of the institution. It took place on 15th September, and Birmingham again poured its tens of thousands into the noble park. A contemperary report says: "from the corner of Dale End to the park, the road was one continued procession of cabs, carts and omnibuses, four abreast". The total number of visitors was estimated at little less than 90,000. £1,700 was handed over on account to the hospital and the rest was divided between the two hospitals.

ILLUS:- POSTCARD OF THE GREAT WESTERN
ARCADE.

THE GREAT WESTERN ARCADE

In 1876, the Great Western Arcade was erected over the tunnel of the Great Western Railway, from Monmouth Street to Temple Row. A company was formed in 1875 to erect the Arcade from plans and designs by Mr W H Ward. The Arcade was lightened up for the first time, on 19th September, 1876, in the presence of the Major, Alderman Baker, and other gentlemen. There were forty-two shops on the ground floor, and a similar number of the balcony, the latter used chiefly as offices. Nearly every artistic trade was represented.

The shop fronts were in ebony and gold, as were the railings of the balcony, and other fittings and the roof and the interior were in etched glass, with the dome in the centre of the building, 75 feet in height from the floor. The wood-work of the roof and the interior of the dome was richly decorated. The arcade was 400 feet long, quite wide, and 40 feet in height to the centre of the arched roof. The galleries were illuminated by the forty-four four-light candelabra and the lower part was lit by the same number of three-light pendants. From the centre of the dome was suspended a massive chandelier, 14 feet high and 8 feet in diameter, comprising two teirs of lights. The Arcade was lighted by 350 lamps, each encased with opal globes, shedding a mellow light on the building, with magnificent effect when they were all lit. The cost of the entire building amounted to nearly £70,000.

HOMEOPATHY

Homeopathy was first introduced into Birmingham in 1845; a Dispensary was opened in Great Charles Street in the same year, but larger and more convenient premises being required, a house in the Old Square was opened as a Homeopathic Hospital and Dispensary in May, 1847.

EARLY SUFFERINGS OF THE QUAKERS

Mr William White's volume "Friends in Warwickshire in the 17th and 18th Centuries" gave a few facts about the early history of the Quakerism in Birmingham. George Fox, the founder of the Society, held a meeting in Birmingham in 1667. During the same decade, at a meeting held at the house of William Reynolds, the following occurred:-

"....a constable came with a rude multitude, armed with swords and staves, who pulled friends out of the house, and beat and abused some of them; they also broke the windows of the house in the constables presence".

"A VERY WATERY TOWN"

Lench's Trust was set up to repair the ruinous ways and bridges of Birmingham, which were numerous. Camden described Birmingham as "very watery". Few towns were more so; the parish comprised, or covered, a hill between two hills, and its two main streams - the Rea and Hockley Brook, had numerous small rivulets or streams for feeders. The great fall of the slope from Hollway Head and Bells Barn gave Clay Brook and Pudding Brook running to the Moat; that from Broad Street, Easy Hill and Paradise Street, a stream by the Parsonage, near Lady Well, swelled by that spring.

The high ground occupied by St Philip's Church drained through Cherry Orchard, across High Street, and formed a stream called "Hassam's ditch". The Priory

Grounds, of great extent and traditionally well wooded, washed down to the Butt's, across the Dale (Dale End) on towards Park Street and through Lake Meadow where it was joined by "Hassam's ditch" and ran past the Bull's Head across Digbeth, dividing the Parish from Aston.

The surface waters of one side of the hill gave bridges to repair and fords to be maintained at Dudley Street, The Parsonage, Edgbaston Street, Moor Street, Park Street, and Dale End. The waters on the other side of the slope through the New Hall estate formed the pool recorded by Water Street, then flowed across Snow Hill, and Walmer Lane, with a bridge and ford at each; others again were found at the Sandpits at Hockley, Aston, Bounbrook, Watery Lane, Lawley Street, a very ancient road and at other points.

Gravel and stones were purchased from Winson Green, and carters labourers, and pavers were constantly employed. Timber was largely used in staking up rude footpaths, and now and again, a bridge was washed away in a flood. The badly-made roads were in hilly situations such as Digbeth and Carr's Lane, easily destroyed by heavy rains. Contract work was unknown – every job was ordered and paid for in detail, even to the ale which was an invariable accompaniment to the work.

THE FEMALE BLONDIN

A woman named Powell, who styled herself "The Female Blondin" was engaged to perform at Aston Park on the high rope in 1863. During the performance, the rope broke and the poor woman was killed instantaneously. Considerable excitement prevailed, and not a little indignation at the action of the hirers in this pandering to the taste for such demoralising exhibitions. This was heightened by the receipt of a letter addressed to the Mayor by the command of the Queen expressing "her personal feelings of horror that one of her subjects – a female – should have been sacrificed to the gratification of the demoralising taste for "such exhibitions". She hoped the Mayor would prevent in future the degradation of such exhibitions of the park which was gladly opened by Her Majesty and the Prince Consort.

This unfortunate occurrence was partly instrumental in bringing about the acquisition of the hall and park by the Town Council.

A CHARITABLE SIDE...

During the seventeenth and eighteenth centuries, the progress of Birmingham manufactures was marvellous. The town attacted artisans of every trade and every degree of skill. Although not situated on any of the great highways of the land, it was easily accessible. It awarded freedom to all who chose to come, Dissenters and Quakers were welcomed. Every man was free to come and go in trade, the system of apprenticeship was only partially known, and Birmingham became emphatically the town of "free trade" where practically no restrictions were known. Coal and iron were easily obtainable from the growing mines and iron works of Staffordshire, and the numerous water mills, and the central position of the town afforded the rapid expansion of the hardware trades.

In their prosperity, the people of Birmingham do not seem to have been deaf to the cries for help which came to them from their suffering brethren in various parts of the country. From "The Town Book" discovered in St Martin's Church during demolition are a number of interesting extracts dating from 1676 to the close of the seventeenth century.

On June 6th, 1679, £2 18s was "collected for a fier at Weedon Northampton Sheer and for Lorgyou in the South of Wilts".

On 2nd May, 1680, £1 6s 5d was collected for "Sufferers by a fier at Wolston" and on 30th May a similar sum was collected for "Sufferers by ffyre at Edghill in the county of Salop".

Fires seem to have been numerous at that time, and it appears that appeals to the people of Birmingham were never in vain. Other entries included sums collected for fires around the country. Perhaps the reason for this special commiseration felt by townsmen for all sufferers by fire may be that they had not forgotten their own sufferings when Prince Rupert torched Birmingham.

THE STRUGGLE FOR FREEDOM

The united political action of the people of Birmingham may be said to have commenced in 1812, and originated in the perils of their trade, threatened, in the first instance, by the renewal of the East Indian Company's Charter, and second, by the promulgation of the Orders in Council, reporting upon Napoleon the Berlin decrees, which crippled the commerce of the country. The people of Birmingham protested against the commercial policy of the Government and 16,000 or more people signed the petition.

Two young men addressed meetings, whose names were destined to become engraven in the history of their town – Thomas Attwood and Richard Spooner. They were chosen to make representation to the Government. When they succeeded in obtaining the revocation of the Orders in Council, they then addressed the vexed issue of the Charter of the East

Indian Company.

They succeeded in breaking The Company's Monopoly in three quarters of the globe. Prior to this, no Englishman was allowed to double the Cape of Good Hope or Cape Horn without the license of the East Indian Company; nor was he allowed to navigate any of the seas between those limits, including the whole of the Pacific Ocean, without a similar license.

This led to the formation of the first political organisation in the town. A group calling themselves the Hampton Club determined to struggle for Parliamentary Reform. The Club was compelled at first to meet in public houses:- The Saracen's Head, Snow Hill, The Nag's Head in Navigation Street, and the Roebuck in Cox Street. Eventually they obtained the use of a private house in Peck Lane. They were looked upon with suspicion by those in authority, as seditious and dangerous. They conducted opposition to the Corn Laws on strictly Constitutional principals. A petition was drawn up on 8th March, 1815 and in less than 24 hours, 48,600 people had signed their names, almost the whole of Birmingham.

The distress continued and in 1826, people were growing disaffected. Soup was distributed, and large sums were subscribed for the relief of the poor, along with words to irritate the disaffected classes. A printer recommended patience which gave people the impression that he had stated that nine shillings a week was sufficient for the support of a man, his wife, and six children.

The magistrates used the Riot Act and Military Aid to preserve public peace, and a troop of 2,000 soldiers were encamped at Sutton Coldfield and remained there for several months, ready to act in case of sudden emergency. There was a crackdown on political men and their clubs. The only place left to meet was in the open air and the first open-air political demonstration took place on Newhall Hill which became consecrated to the great struggle for freedom, as an arena for free debate, a spot which became the scene of some of the most noteworthy events in the history of the 19th century.

A TERRIBLE ACCIDENT

In August, 1823, occurred a terrible accident in Birmingham. In St Mary's Square a tremendous explosion could be heard some distance away. The effects in the immediate vicinity greatly resembled the slight shock of an earthquake. The explosion occurred on the premises of Mr Wilson, formerly of Messrs. Wilson, Starkey & Co., button makers. In a back room, or warehouse adjoining the house, the body of Mr Wilson was discovered, almost entirely buried beneath a heap of rubbish, shockingly mutilated and disfigured, and deprived of all signs of life; and in other parts of the same room, but at some distance, one of the females employed in the manufactory was found expiring from the effects of the injury she had sustained. The room where the bodies were found was almostly completely ruined – the floor, ceiling, walls and roof were damaged, and a large counter was forced through an aperture into a workshop beneath.

In an adjoining room, several females were at work, two of whom were seriously injured and two others slightly so. The explosion was caused by gunpowder, or so it was thought and a large crowd gathered to the spot.

It later appeared that Mr Wilson, aged 21, had been manufacturing percussion or fulminating powder – a chemical compound of highly dangerous preparation. It was some consolation to know that the deaths of the sufferers must have been almost instantaneous. A verdict of Accidental Death was returned.

THE REMOVAL OF THE TURN-PIKE AT DERITEND

A welcome reform was the removal of the turnpike gate in Deritend in 1828. In 1787, an act was passed to erect a Turnpike at Deritend Bridge, for the purpose of taking down and rebuilding the bridge, for widening the avenues there to, and for preventing the lower part of the town from being overflowed.

At this period, in times of flood, the lower part of Digbeth was impassible, and it became absolutely necessary to take down and rebuild the bridge, and to widen, deepen, and vary the bed and course of the river. The small toll of 2d for every four-wheeled carriage, 1d for every two-wheeled carriage and ½d for every horse was to be sufficient in the course of four years to enable the Trustees to take down and rebuild the bridge, and make every other necessary improvement. The amount collected during the four years, however, produced only £500 per annum which was only half of the estimated amount. An application to increase the tolls was unsuccessful, and later the turnpike was removed altogether.

THE BIRMINGHAM RAILWAYS

People were inclined to believe in the new engines of locomotives which could travel twice as fast as stage coaches, but also imagined all sorts of difficulties. In rural districts they were afraid that the smoke of the iron horse may injure the fleeces of the sheep, or that of an occasional straying cow would prove an awkward obstacle for the train. Others feared that the sparks from the engine should set fire to the adjoining properties along the line.

In 1832, the country was astonished by the proposal to construct a railway from London to Birmingham, for which a Bill was introduced. The Bill passed through the Commons but was rejected by the Lords. The application was removed in 1833.

In June 1834, the work of constructing the line was commenced, and was successfully completed in about four years – a work involving almost one third more labour than did the construction of the Great Pyramid of Cheops, and which necessitated the removal of as much material as would encompass the earth more than three times with a band one foot high and three feet broad. However, this was not the first line to be opened. Another line was completed 14 months earlier in 1834, that from Birmingham to Manchester, to be called the Grand Junction Railway.

The Birmingham Journal describes the opening scene on July 4th:-

"At 7 o clock precisely in the morning, the bell rang, when the opening train, drawn by the 'Wildfire' engine, commenced moving. The train consisted of eight carriages, all of the first class, and bearing the following names: Greyhound, Swallow, Liverpool and Birmingham Mail, Celerity, Umpire, Statesman, and Birmingham and Manchester Mail! The train started slowly; but emerging from the yard (at Vauxhall) speedily burst off at a rapid rate. To those who for the first time witnessed such a scene it was peculiarly exciting, and the immense multitude, as far as the eye could reach, gave expression to their admiration by loud and long-continued huzzas, and the waving of hats and handkerchiefs."

The people soon became accustomed to the new mode of travelling and later railway developments caused considerably less excitement. One of the favourite hobbies of inventors and engineers was to construct an engine which would run on common roads and one of the most successful of these projects was the steam coach by the celebrated Dr Church, a resident in Birmingham. This vehicle, which carried 40 people, was used in the streets of Birmingham in 1833.

ALL SAINT'S CHURCH

In the 1830s, the first church to be built by private enterprise was All Saints, erected on what was then known only as Birmingham Heath, Although it was the centre of what was already becoming a very largely populated district, promising soon to connect the Midland metropolis with the great "black country" beyond. All Saints was built in Gothic style and cost £3,817.

We have travelled through centuries of Birmingham life, and have traced her growth from the cradle. The Birmingham man (or woman!) may claim with truth to be a citizen of "no mean city".

It is no small honour that I am able to stand among the worthies of the city and be able to say: "I, too, am a Birmingham man".